Rotary

This book donated by

The Rotary Club of Evanston

The Spirit of
Flamenco

The Spirit of Flamenco

From Spain to New Mexico
By Nicolasa Chávez

Museum of New Mexico Press
Santa Fe

Contents

Preface

One may wonder why the Museum of International Folk Art, with a mission to foster an understanding of traditions and cultures around the world as they existed in the past and have evolved into the present, decided to mount an exhibition on the subject of flamenco. In fact, when I suggested the exhibition concept to the museum, a former co-worker asked, "Isn't flamenco a performance art?" To which I responded, "That is exactly why the museum needs to have an exhibition on flamenco."

Flamenco is very much a living folkloric tradition apart from the staged performance aspect with which it is largely associated. Originally performed among families hidden away in the caves of Andalusia, it transformed into a performance art in the small *cafés cantantes* (singing cafés) of the nineteenth century and eventually moved to large theater stages. These new manifestations did not diminish the earlier customs, however. Today, traditional flamenco still exists as a way of life for the people of southern Spain and for groups in other parts of the country. Any student or aficionado recognizes that to truly understand flamenco and its place within the wider family of Spanish dance, it is critical to travel to southern Spain and to breathe the air that gave life to this art form.

The museum provides the perfect setting for exploring the evolving manifestations of flamenco: from its traditional roots among the Gypsies in Spain to its popularity in the United States and its prevalence in the cultural landscape of New

Pareja de Baile (Dance Partners) by José García Ramos,
1884-86. Oil on linen, 21⁶/₁₀ x 14½ in.

Mexico. This exhibition focuses on the folkloric roots of flamenco and then traces its history as it transformed into a performance art. Of particular interest are public fiestas and ferias in both Spain and New Mexico in which flamenco and Spanish dance, both classical and folkloric, are featured. The story of flamenco in New Mexico unfolds from its beginnings at the popular El Nido restaurant in Tesuque during the 1960s to the renowned Festival Flamenco Internacional de Albuquerque. The exhibition includes costumes, guitars, album covers, photographs, fine art, ephemera, and video—all of which combine to tell the rich history of flamenco dance and music in the state.

The Museum of International Folk Art and other New Mexico museums are not strangers to the traditions and customs of flamenco. Festivals, performances, lectures, and demonstrations were held at several of the state's institutions as early as the 1960s. One of the first performances took place in 1963 at St. Francis Auditorium under the auspices of the Museum of Fine Arts (now the New Mexico Museum of Art). Produced by dancer Vicente Romero, the performance followed his sojourn in Spain and touring with the world-renowned company of José Greco. It was accompanied by guitarists Hector García and Luís Campos and would be the first of numerous shows of traditional flamenco put on by Romero. Until this time, New Mexican audiences were accustomed to a hybridization of folkloric and classical Spanish music, often referred to as the *aflamencado* style. The owner of El Nido, Ray Arias, who was seated in the audience, was mesmerized by what he saw and subsequently began a partnership with Romero that gave birth to the flamenco scene in Northern New Mexico.[1]

Three years later, in 1966, the Museum of International Folk Art hosted Romero in a performance that included guitarist René Heredia and singer Miguel Galvez, both Gypsies from Spain. This was followed by a performance at St. Francis Auditorium during the Fiesta de Santa Fe with guest artist Lydia Torea, a dancer of half-Spanish, half-Polish decent from Phoenix, Arizona. The program proved so popular that two performances were scheduled for the 1967 fiestas. This second rendition included guitarists René Heredia and Miguel Romero (Vicente's brother), dancer Carla Duran of Santa Fe, and the duo of Choly and Isabel from Spain.

Periodic performances and demonstrations in New Mexico museums continued for more than two decades, including two 1985 performances by Luís Campos and his wife, dancer Lili del Castillo, at the Museum of International Folk Art. The shows, one for a general audience and the other for children and families, celebrated the opening of the exhibition *Vivan las Fiestas*. The performances also kicked off the artist-in-residency program of Campos and Castillo, which took their flamenco lectures and demonstrations across the entire state. In 1988 the Palace of the Governors, now the New Mexico History Museum and Palace of the Governors, hosted a gathering of flamenco artists and groups from Santa Fe and Albuquerque. Set up in the courtyard of the historic building, the event showcased more than twenty artists, all New Mexicans who had at one time or another lived and studied in Spain. Reminiscent of the shows held in the perfumed courtyards of Andalusia, the performance ended with an informal *juerga* (jam session) under a starry sky.

In the 1980s, New Mexico was known as a flamenco mecca. It was home to one of the earliest US flamenco festivals, hosted by the University of New Mexico, which also offered one of the first degree programs with an emphasis in flamenco. A summer itinerary for tourists and aficionados interested in New Mexico's multicultural art and history included visits to pueblos such as Acoma, the state's fabulous museums, and parks such as Bandelier, followed by an evening at the Santa Fe Opera or a flamenco show. This presence in New Mexico has led to the popular misconception that flamenco came to the state along the Camino Real with the Spanish conquistadores and friars. Quite fantastical is the image of a seventeenth-century caravan with equestrian men in armor and a band of Gypsy women in ruffled dresses carrying castanets. Even though New Mexico's Hispano roots date back more than 400 years, flamenco is a relative newcomer to the cultural milieu of New Mexico.

As a child, I also believed that flamenco was always a part of my New Mexican heritage. I grew up seeing performances by María Benítez's Teatro Flamenco and taking lessons with Vicente Romero, never knowing a time when flamenco did not exist in the state. After returning from a year in Spain, I heard about the Festival Flamenco Internacional de Albuquerque. I began attending each year, took more classes, and began my own flamenco journey, learning from teachers and aficionados that, more than a dance or musical tradition, flamenco is a way of life. Why has this way of life, so natural in Spain, become such a fixture in New Mexico? Why do New Mexicans feel such resonance with flamenco dance, music, and emotions, and why do they feel a common bond with its country of origin? For those who have traveled and studied in Spain, who then come to the state and make it their home, the common response is, "It feels like being back in Spain." The presence of flamenco and the continued use of the Spanish language has added to the draw.

Artistic collaborations between local performers and those from out of state have helped the tradition develop into what we know and experience today. This book and the exhibition provide a glimpse into the rich history of flamenco and its transference to New Mexico. I hope that they also honor the people who brought flamenco to the state and made the flamenco community what it is today.

Prologue

Passionate, fiery, sensual, intense—these are some of the adjectives used to describe flamenco's highly expressive dance and music. In the United States, when one thinks of flamenco, images of a dark-haired female dancer and men in *torero* costumes immediately come to mind, along with jugs of sangria, steaming paella, and bowls of chilled gazpacho.

These delicacies are iconic offerings of the country of Spain, but most have origins in particular regions. Traditional paella comes from Valencia, while gazpacho is from Andalusia. The same holds true for flamenco. Even though it has become one of the most recognizable art forms associated with Spain, visitors to the majority of the country's regions discover that flamenco is rare or nonexistent in the local nightclubs or dinner theaters. On the other hand, while walking down the street during a local fiesta a visitor might experience a joyous regional dance, such as the *jota*, or some other village favorite. In Spain, flamenco is synonymous with the region of Andalusia, and while it does enjoy popularity in other regions and larger cities it is not the most common form of music or dance.

The often misguided impression that flamenco is the quintessence of Spain is largely the product of late eighteenth and early nineteenth-century travel writers, whose romanticism led to idealistic interpretations of the country. These writings

La Chunga, 1964. Photograph by Colita. This dancer's performances at Madrid's famous Café de Chinitas epitomized the ravishing, passionate Gypsy. Several dancers from the United States began their careers performing with her while they studied in Madrid.

Gitanos, Granada, Spain, c. 1900. Photograph by Rafael Garzón Rodríguez. Photographs such as these were staged for a tourist audience. Often the models were a mix of Gypsy and non-Gypsy people in classic flamenco poses.

conjured an exotic Spain populated with bullfighters and dark-skinned enchant-resses and passionate Gypsies, who danced and sang late into the night. One of the most popular of these writers was the American Washington Irving, who in 1829 took up residence in the Barrio Santa Cruz in Seville, where he wrote his famous *Tales of the Alhambra* (1832). In 1843, the French poet and novelist Théophile Gautier promoted the beauty of Spanish dancers in his travelogue *Voyage en Espagne (Tra los Montes)*. The British writer Richard Ford followed shortly after with his 1845 guidebook for travelers, *Gatherings from Spain*. One year later, in 1846, a novella came out that would spread the image of the enticing, passionate Gypsy woman to romantics around the world. The French historian and writer Prosper Mérimée's *Carmen* forever engraved the image of the dark-skinned beauty in the minds and hearts of millions. The book was adapted as an opera by the French composer Georges Bizet in 1875. To this day, *Carmen* is one of the most popular operas of all time, fueling a hunger for all things expressing the essence of Spain and flamenco. But deeper than the mythology is the living folkloric tradition we will explore in these pages.

Chapter 1

The Birth and Development of the Flamenco Tradition

To many around the world, flamenco is a dramatic, national art form performed in a theater by traveling dance companies. In reality, flamenco is a regional art form, handed down from generation to generation, and originally performed only within families or tight-knit communities. It is one tradition within a larger family of Spanish dances that can be divided into four distinct categories: flamenco, the *escuela bolera*, folkloric/regional dances, and the *estilo Andaluz*.[1]

Escuela bolera is a classical style that developed during the eighteenth century and shares characteristics with Italian and French ballet of the era. However, the bolero style incorporates distinctly Iberian characteristics, including erect posture, extension of the arms, intricate footwork, and high leaps, along with playing castanets. Because many of the steps are similar to classical ballet, the dancer wears soft slippers.

The folkloric genre comprises dances and music from the fifty provinces. One such dance is the jota, which, like many folkloric dances, varies in style from region to region. Aragón, in northeastern Spain, has become famous for its version, and the *jota Aragonesa* is performed in many shows of Spanish dance. The folkloric Andalusian dances and songs include the *malagueñas, seguidillas, panaderos,* and

José Greco, the American star of Spanish dance, poses in a publicity shot with his second wife and partner, Lola de Ronda, c. 1950–1951. They are in costume for the *escuela bolera*. The costumes are based on the bullfighter's outfit and eighteenth-century countryside dress. The soft-soled slippers are used in place of heeled shoes.

Alpargatas (espadrilles) made for regional dances in Trujilllo, Spain, 2012. Cotton, jute, rubber. These special shoes are common elements of regional costumes throughout Spain.

opposite:
Contemporary costume for spring village dances in the town of Trujillo, Extremadura, Spain, 2012. Skirt and waste purse by Guadalupe Costa Barrado; vest, top, petticoat, bloomers by María Bravo García and Amparo Jiménez; apron and patterns for skirt and waist purse by Antonio Rodríguez Lebrón. Wool felt, cotton, nylon, satin, metal.

fandangos. These dances are similar to flamenco in their torso carriage (holding the rib cage and chest high with the shoulders down and slightly back), small amounts of percussive footwork, fluid arm movements, and *floreo,* which are hand movements that create a motion reminiscent of flowers and leaves flowing through the air. The styles and movements of these dances influenced and were influenced by flamenco, and some of the more popular forms have been incorporated into flamenco's repertoire.

Like the Andalusian regional dances, flamenco comes from Spain's southernmost region. Historians and scholars have narrowed down its origins to the "flamenco triangle," which is the area between the cities of Seville, Cádiz, and Jerez

Skirt used for dancing the *jota Legarterana*, c. 1960s. Felt, cotton, satin, metallic thread. The *jota* is danced throughout the country, with its name and costume styles varying slightly from region to region. This costume is used in the town of Legartera in the region of Castilla–La Mancha.

opposite:
Male costume for dancing the *jota Aragonesa*, c. 1970s. Cotton, wool. The *jota Aragonesa* is the most popular of the regional versions of this dance. This costume is typical of the attire worn by men both in Aragón and for staged productions.

0   100   200   300 Miles

0   100   200   300 Kilometers

CANTÁBRIAS

BASQUE PROVINCES

LA RIOJA

FRANCE

ASTURIAS

GALICIA

NAVARRE

Girona •

CATALONIA

Barcelona ✪
    • Montjuic

CASTILLE AND LEÓN

ARAGÓN

ATLANTIC OCEAN

PORTUGAL

MADRID

✪ Madrid

Legartera •

CASTILLE LA MANCHA

VALENCIA

Trujillo •

◉ Mérida

• Campo de Criptana

EXTREMADURA

SEA

BALEARIC ISLANDS

◉ Córdoba

Murcia ✪

MURCIA

MEDITERRANEAN

• Cartagena

ANDALUSIA

Huelva •

Seville ✪

Ronda •

◉ Granada

Almería ◉

Flamenco Triangle (Cradle of Flamenco)

Cádiz ◉

• Málaga

Jerez de la Frontera

Strait of Gibraltar   • Ceuta

ALGERIA

• Melilla

N

MOROCCO

To the **CANARY ISLANDS**

Legend	
—·—·—	Countries
········	Regions
✪	National capital
✪	Regional capital
◉	Provincial capital
•	City or town

de la Frontera (often referred to as simply Jerez). But other pockets in the Andalusian countryside, including Granada, are also considered home to flamenco. Various genres within Andalusian dance and flamenco are named after the regions from which they developed. For example, the *murcianas* come from Murcia and the *rondeñas* from Ronda. The malagueña is an example of a regional Andalusian dance that became so imbued with a flamenco sound that it is now considered part of the larger family tree of flamenco. Another is the *fandango de Huelva*, a folk dance dating back to Phoenician times. It has strong flamenco characteristics yet contains smooth melodic tones that show off the voice. The fandango is one of the most popular flamenco genres, and more than 150 varieties of the song exist.[2]

LAMENTATIONS: GITANO ROOTS

In the historical discourse on flamenco there is considerable debate regarding the amount of mixing that took place between regional dance and music, the various cultures of Spain, and traditions perceived as of pure Gitano (Gypsy) origin.[3] Generally, history holds that flamenco was developed in the mountain caves of Andalusia by Gitanos shortly after they were expelled by the Catholic monarchs Ferdinand and Isabella at the end of the fifteenth century. The recently married rulers united the kingdoms of Castile and León and issued an edict in 1492 in an effort to cleanse the newly formed Spanish empire of minority groups. Jews, Muslims, and Gitanos were told to convert to Christianity or face expulsion from the country. Some of these people did leave Spain; others hid in caves. The first examples of what is known as flamenco's deep song, or *cante jondo*, stem from these expelled peoples. Their early songs, often referred to as "cries" or "laments," tell stories of pain, loss, suffering, displacement, death, and heartache. They are more somber than the regional musical traditions and are considered to be the oldest, purest, and most profound of flamenco songs.

Today most flamencologists and ethnomusicologists agree that the historic roots of flamenco date back even further than the fifteenth century and that Spain's plethora of rich cultures contributed to its early development. In historic Spain, the roots of flamenco are in the south in what would become Andalusia. The earliest mentions of a musical style particular to the Iberian Peninsula can be traced to the Phoenician colony of Gades (present-day Cádiz). From there, the earliest spread of Andalusian dance and music took place during the first century CE. The region passed to Carthaginian control and eventually became a part of the Roman Empire at the beginning of the second century CE. It is believed that young female dancers accompanied travelers back to Rome during this time. The Byzantine Empire controlled the Mediterranean coast from Cádiz to Valencia from around 480 CE until the Muslim takeover in 711 CE. Spain then became a Moorish stronghold for nearly 800 years. During the medieval era, Spain began its long-standing heritage of cultural blending. Christian, Arabic, and Jewish cultures shared their musical traditions. It is generally believed that the first Gitanos arrived during this time as camp followers of the invading Islamic forces, bringing with them the cultures of India, Eastern Europe, and the Byzantine Empire and influences from their travels throughout the Arab world. The sounds and techniques of all these musical traditions mixed with those of southern Spain.

Despite this mingling, flamenco came to represent a specific group of people and incorporates an appreciation of their culture, history, and heritage. The life experience of the people of southern Spain, the Gitanos in particular, is the most important aspect of the art form. Along with the sadness and seriousness of cante jondo, flamenco is also imbued with a sense of pride and the desire to live free. It reflects the sentiments of a people traveling from land to land in search of home, a people accustomed to living on the outskirts of society in the open *campo* (countryside). Even though Gitanos and non-Gitanos alike enjoy and take part in flamenco, for the Gitanos flamenco has become a way of life. Families, relatives close and distant, and community members interact through song, music, and dance. Flamenco is often considered an outward expression of one's innermost emotions, whether happy or sad, and carries an air of freedom or abandon. Originally, flamenco was not performed before an audience, and *flamencos*, those who are part of the flamenco community, were not professional performers but everyday people.[4] Even today, a passerby walking down the street may hear an impromptu song or witness teenagers clapping their hands in unison or bouncing counter-rhythms off one another.

The prominent display of raw emotion is referred to as *duende*, a term coined by writer Federico García Lorca. The concept of duende also refers to the passionate, trance-like state of being totally immersed in song and dance. Duende is not specific to the family of cante jondo and can appear in many forms, including happiness, sorrow, pride, and even a touch of humor—light or dark—along with biting sarcasm. The unabashed and instinctual display of intense feelings is part of what makes flamenco so memorable to outsiders, especially those who are reluctant to expose their emotions for all to see.

OPENING UP THE CIRCLE: THE GOLDEN ERA

Flamenco was originally a folkloric tradition, shared between family and community members and most often performed in a confined space. Typically, both common and festive flamenco take place with a group of people sitting or standing in a circle. The participants in the outer ring clap their hands to provide the rhythm for those taking turns dancing in the center. Musicians play their guitars, and singers take turns accompanying the music. The dancer in the center controls the situation by using body movements to manipulate the mood, rhythm, and speed of the music and song, projecting that energy to the entire group, and each of those people then react to the movements, signs, and so on. This communication makes flamenco a communal experience that is also passed from one family member and

Gypsies partying in the Montjuïc area of Barcelona, 1963. Photograph by Colita. This unscripted scene dispels the popular myth that flamenco dance and music only represent sadness and anguish. Festivals and family gatherings included flamenco to express joy and to share playfulness, with members of the community calling and responding to each other.

Fernanda (in striped blouse) and Bernarda de Utrera, 1969. Photograph by Colita. These two famous sisters from the town of Utrera outside Seville are the most popular female duo in the history of flamenco song.

A Gypsy girl learning the art of flamenco from her elders, Campo de Criptam, Castilla la Mancha, 1963. Photograph by Colita.

The *café cantante* El Burrero was one of the most popular
flamenco cafés in Seville in the late nineteenth century.
This interior shot shows a traditional *cuadro* (group) on stage,
c. 1880. Photograph by Emilio Beauchy.

generation to the next. Younger flamencos express themselves through fast footwork and intricate movements, while those less agile use facial expressions and
body line. No matter how it is danced, sung, or played, flamenco is a centuries-old
expression of a people and their way of life. The phenomenon of foreigners learning the dance and music in academies is relatively new.

Around the turn of the nineteenth century various factors contributed to the
transformation of flamenco from a private tradition into a public performance art.
The first was the 1782 Leniency Edict of Charles III, which eliminated the long-
standing persecution of the Gitanos, permitting the acceptance of their traditions
and culture. In 1808, the invasion of Spain by Napoleon's forces prompted an anti-
France sentiment. The resistance to everything French led to the adaptation and
acceptance of regional Spanish folk culture. The upper classes embraced *costumbrismo*, incorporating folkloric traditions, costumes, music, and dance into their
daily lives.[5] Finally, throughout Western Europe the advent of a middle class and
newly moneyed families led to an influx of thrill-seeking tourists and travel writers
in search of exotic experiences.

By the late 1840s, flamencos began sharing their art in public forums, especially at cafés cantantes. These cafés were the first venues in Spain to provide live

variety theater. In addition to flamenco, there were animal shows and comedy acts, most of which were local or regional performers. The café cantante reached its height in 1880 with the opening of what became the most prestigious café of the era: El Burrero, founded by impresario and singer Silverio Franconetti. He made flamenco the main attraction, replacing the escuela bolera, which had been considered the national dance of Spain. The flamenco performances were saved for each evening's grand finale, and they often turned into late-night jam sessions, or juergas, that lasted into the morning hours. The opening of hundreds of additional cafés cantantes, where flamencos were paid for their work, allowed practitioners to become professional artists.

The period of the café cantante is referred to as flamenco's "golden era." The transformation of a familial tradition into a respected art form, admired and accepted by Spaniards and foreigners alike, did not go unnoticed. The stars of the cafés cantantes between 1880 and 1900 became known for their signature dances or songs. They were immortalized in publications and enjoyed enthusiastic audiences. These performers were the pioneers who shaped how we view, experience, and understand flamenco today.

Baile por Bulerías (Dancing to Bulerías) by José García Ramos, 1884. Oil on linen, 20½ x 11 in. The Seville painter José García Ramos rose to popularity during the late nineteenth century at the height of the *costumbrismo* movement, when local and and regional dress and costume styles were favored over the contemporary styles of France. García Ramos painted the local flamencos and Gypsies as dressed for performance or special outings. This couple is dressed for a *fiesta de bulerías* (a party or jam session in the wildly expressive *bulerías* style).

In the cafés, instead of performing in a circle the guitarists, singers, and dancers sat in a semicircle facing the audience. Dancers took turns performing their solos in front of the semicircle. Those who were not front and center accompanied the dancer with rhythmic hand clapping and enthusiastic shouts of encouragement, referred to as *jaleos*. The convention of jaleo is quite foreign to audiences unaccustomed to traditional flamenco, in which older generations shouted out words of encouragement to the young and vice versa. This was viewed as a way for younger family members to learn from their elders and share a communal space in which to experiment and grow. The cafés cantantes opened up the circle to include audience members, and those familiar with flamenco shouted jaleos of "bien hecho," "guapa," "asi se baila," "asi se toca," and "olé"—much to the excitement or dismay of tourists seated nearby.[6]

Whether accepted by the tourist or not, the passionate and often loud interactions between dancers, musicians, and spectators are part of the shared experience. The performer controls the situation, drawing in the spectator, who participates in the show at the dancer's whim. This audience-performer dynamic can be seen in many artworks of the era, including those of American expatriate John Singer Sargent, who spent time in Spain when Franconetti's café was still open. Sargent's *The Spanish Dance* (1880) and *Spanish Dancer* (1882), a study for his more famous *El Jaleo* (1882), are timeless examples of performers who are larger than life. Sargent's dancers draw the viewer into the setting, and one can almost feel the music. Like the romantic writings from the early and mid-nineteenth century, these paintings have shaped popular conceptions of the shared flamenco experience.

PRESERVATION: ADAPTATION AND COLLABORATION

At the end of the nineteenth century, Spain's performance venues began to make use of the technological changes sweeping the globe, such as electric lighting, sound recording, photography, and film. Life in larger cities changed at a rapid pace, and more modern venues based on European-style cabarets, variety theaters, and music halls were introduced. These establishments were spacious and provided multi-use spaces for different types of variety shows, which were referred to as *variedades*. These shows, which included foreign performers, featured young, scantily clad singers, a chorus line of dancers, and circus acts. Each show ended with orchestral social dances, such as the fox-trot and the Argentine tango, both popular after their introduction in France. Late-night social dancing pushed flamenco out of the spotlight as an evening's finale, and juergas moved into the homes of wealthy aficionados who paid flamencos to perform for their private parties.

Variedades led to the eventual decline of the cafés cantantes. For a while they coexisted, with the cafés providing a multigenerational experience, while the European cabarets catered to a younger audience. The cafés cantantes died out sooner in

The Spanish Dance by John Singer Sargent,
c. 1880. Oil on canvas, 35¼ x 33¼ in.

the larger cities of Madrid and Barcelona. In the south, the birthplace of flamenco, the introduction of the variedades met with resistance. As late as 1914 the café El Kursaal Central attempted to congregate the best flamenco artists of the era. Artists performing classical flamenco enjoyed this venue, while others attempted to perform in the variedades and music halls alongside the European acts. Some complained of being relegated to the opening act, when the venue was half full; others felt that the new venues infused flamenco with a breath of fresh air. One of the aspects of any traditional folk art is its living adaptability to new environments, and flamenco adapted to the forces of modernity, both positive and negative.

Spanish Dancer by John Singer Sargent, 1882. Watercolor,
11¹³⁄₁₆ x 7⅞. These paintings reveal a romantic fascination with
Spanish dance shared by many non-Spanish artists of the period.

At this time, major efforts to preserve traditional flamenco began. Ironically, among the greatest preservationists were the most forward-thinking practitioners in the field. In attempting to preserve a centuries-old tradition, these young professionals utilized new technologies and artistic collaborations to push flamenco and its appreciation to unseen heights. By the 1910s and 1920s, professionals performed in theaters and concert halls usually reserved for *zarzuelas* (operettas) and ballet. At the same time, flamenco became more academic, and members of the educated classes collaborated with local Gitano performers. One of the earliest

Pastora Imperio, c. 1910. Imperio was the first great flamenco star of the early twentieth century. She was of Gypsy descent and not only performed flamenco but was a well-known singer of contemporary Spanish *cuplé*, a popular form of music during the early twentieth century. She starred in many Spanish movies and continued to perform into her sixties.

collaborations involved the Spanish composer Manuel de Falla and Pastora Monje Imperio, a Gitana from a long line of flamenco performers, including her great-aunt La Cuchera and her mother, Rosario Monje, both of whom were famous singers, or *cantaoras*.[7]

Imperio honed her craft, becoming a multitalented performer who was known for singing French versions of *cuplés* (popular songs), as well if not better than any French *variedades* star.[8] Falla was considered the top modernist Spanish composer and was one of the first to incorporate traditional flamenco into classical orchestral productions and ballet. His famous symphonic suite and ballet *El Amor Brujo* (Bewitched Love or Bewitching Love) was created with both Rosario and Pastora in mind.[9] It first premiered as *Embrujo de Sevilla* (Bewitchment from Seville) in 1915 at Teatro Lara in Madrid.

Imperio's performances attracted a younger audience to Spanish dance at the same time that modernist European choreographers and dancers were incorporating folkloric and regional cultural expressions into their productions. Several projects with Spanish themes had dancers and musicians collaborating with modernist and avant-garde artists, including the symbolist Néstor Martín-Fernández de la Torre, the surrealist Salvador Dalí, the multitalented Pablo Picasso, and the Russian modernist Natalia Goncharova. These artists incorporated their modernist techniques into costume and set designs for various productions.

The most famous ballet company to incorporate regional folk culture was the Ballets Russes under the direction of impresario Sergei Diaghilev. Inspired by Imperio's performances in *Gitanería en Dos Cuadros* and a desire to incorporate traditional Spanish dance into his ballets, Diaghilev and Ballets Russes took up residence in Spain in 1913 during the First World War. While there he met with Falla in Granada, then returned in 1916 with dancer and choreographer Léonide Massine to collaborate with Falla on a production of *El Sombrero de Tres Picos* (The Three-Pointed Hat), which premiered at Madrid's Teatro Eslava. It was renamed *El Tricornio* (The Three-Cornered Hat) and presented at the Alhambra Theatre in London in 1919, with décor, set design, backdrop, curtains, and costumes by Picasso.[10] In 1921, Diaghilev returned to Spain, this time hiring local Gitano performers from the café cantante era to produce *Cuadro Flamenco*.[11] It premiered at the Alhambra Theatre in London in 1921, and once again the set and décor were by Picasso. King Alfonso XIII of Spain traveled to London to attend the performance.[12]

As flamenco gained fresh momentum in the theaters and opera houses of Paris and London, practitioners in Spain created a unique format in order to preserve the traditional forms. Perhaps the most important collaboration of the era was the 1922 Primer Concurso del Cante Jondo (First Congress of Cante Jondo) in Granada. The *concurso* (competition), which was the brainchild of Lorca and Falla, brought together the best local and regional cantaores.[13] Andalusian singers, mostly amateurs, from villages and cities large and small descended upon Granada, where they

Poster for the ballet *El Amor Brujo*, 1924, by Manuel de Falla,
text by G. Martínez Sierra. The original production was written
specifically for Pastora Imperio. The ballet debuted in Paris and
became Falla's iconic work.

Mantón de Manila (Manila shawl), Spain or China, early twentieth century. Silk, rayon, synthetic dyes. The Manila shawl originated in China and is named for the Manila galleons that traded between Acapulco and the Philippines. By the beginning of the twentieth century shawls were made in Spain, and they remain synonymous with Spanish fashion today. In flamenco and classical dance the shawl is used in the same manner as a cape, passed around the body and draped to create lines and silhouettes of the female form.

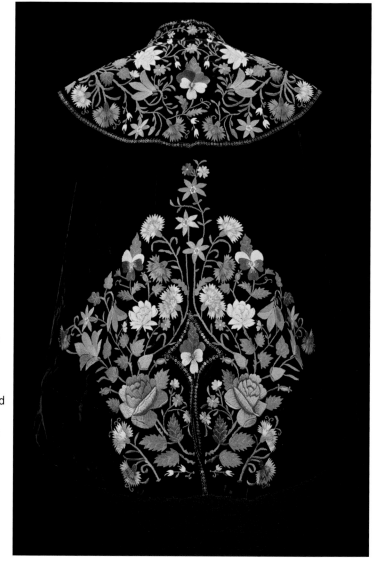

Capote de entrada (bullfighter's entrance cape), Madrid, c. 1960s. Satin, rayon, metal, synthetic dyes. The entrance cape is another element traditionally used in the bullring that has become incorporated into Spanish dance. The dancer manipulates the cape to the rhythm of the music while mimicking steps emblematic of a bullfighter in the ring. Typically used by male dancers, women may also incorporate capes into theatrical pieces.

Bata de cola (flamenco dress with train), Madrid, c. 1960s. Silk, polyester, nylon. Early flamenco costumes developed from the street wear of the late nineteenth century. At the time, *batas* (trains) were a common feature. Dance movements developed to work with them to the music. While the train is no longer ever-present in flamenco, its use requires specialized technique and skill.

Traje de luces (bullfighter's costume), Spain, 1888. The "suit of lights" is one of the most emblematic symbols of Spanish masculinity. The suit is named for its elaborate embroidery, beadwork, and knotting. The outfit, while functional in the bullring, has become customary in classical Spanish dance, while the jacket alone is often used in flamenco performance.

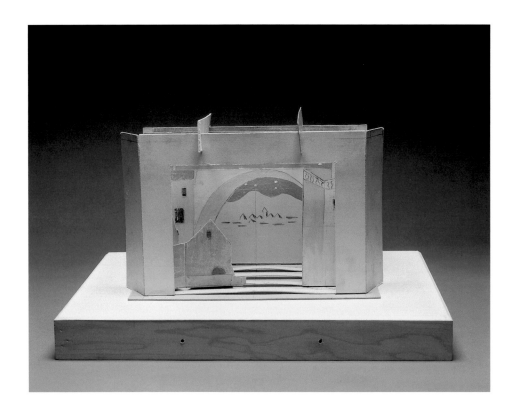

Early maquette for the set of *Le Tricorne (The Three-Cornered Hat)* by Pablo Picasso, 1919. Watercolor, ink, and graphite on board, 6 ¼ x 10 ½ x 5 ½ in.

Fan by Natalia Gontcharova, ca. 1914-16. Gouache on linen, with bamboo and mother of pearl, 9 ½ x 17 x 1 in. (open).

competed with one another before an audience of Gitano and *gachó* (non-Gypsy) aficionados. By showcasing local artists and presenting cante jondo in its purest form, the concurso debuted the work of many flamencos. And rather than singing for a tourist audience, they performed for one another, gaining recognition within the flamenco community. Today, concursos are celebrated throughout Andalusia, serving as forums for preserving the genre.

THE GENERATION OF 1927: LOCALS AND THE AVANT-GARDE

Lorca and Falla were members of the Generation of 1927, a group of influential poets and writers that promoted local traditions, the avant-garde, and collaborative projects that brought flamenco and Gypsy life to the theater. Two artists with whom they collaborated were the dancers Antonia Mercé, popularly known by her stage name, La Argentina, and Encarnación López y Júlvez, known by her stage name,

Antonia Mercé, "La Argentina," 1925. Photograph by Dora Kallmus.

La Argentina (*back to camera*) on the set of her theatrical production *Triana*, which debuted at the Opéra Comique, Paris, in 1929. It was a full-length Spanish ballet with music by Spanish composer Isaac Albéniz and sets and costumes by Néstor, aka Néstor Martín Fernandez de la Torre.

La Argentinita. Despite the similarity of their stage names and the fact that both women were born of Spanish *criollo* (Creole) parents from Argentina, they were not related. La Argentina came from a theatrical family: her father was the principal dancer for Madrid's Teatro Real. From him, she learned classical dance and escuela bolera. La Argentinita learned her first Spanish dances in a Buenos Aires café, and upon her family's return to Spain, she began performing for high-society fiestas. Both women developed an appreciation of traditional flamenco and studied with Gitanos. They were also known as well-rounded, multitalented artists who not only danced but also choreographed, produced, and directed their own shows, often incorporating flamenco and regional dance into their productions.

La Argentina is considered the first modernist flamenca, and she became the voice of a new generation. She left her job as a dancer at the Teatro Real to study traditional flamenco in Andalusia among the Gitanos and with the maestro of castanets, José Otero. Adapting regional Spanish and flamenco dance for large concert halls throughout Europe and the United States, she eventually spread her love of

Pastora Imperio (*center*), Vicente Escudero, and La Argentina on the set of *El Amor Brujo*, 1935.

flamenco and Spanish dance to the farthest reaches of the world, touring Russia, India, Egypt, and Japan. Her first Spanish opera, *El Amor de España* (The Love from Spain), was presented in 1910 at the Moulin Rouge in Paris. She also starred alongside Pastora Imperio and modernist dancer Vicente Escudero in Falla's *Embrujo de Sevilla* (Bewitchment from Seville) at the Alhambra Theatre in London. During the 1920s she gained total artistic control over her own productions and in 1929 began her own company, one of the first to transform Spanish dance from solo work to performance by an ensemble or troupe. She reworked Falla's masterpiece, *El Amor Brujo*, as a ballet and premiered another version as late as 1935, starring once again Pastora Imperio and Vicente Escudero.

La Argentina collaborated with many members of the Generation of 1927, including the classical composers and brothers Rodolfo and Ernesto Halffter, both disciples of Falla, and María Teresa Prieto. She received wide acclaim and respect among her contemporaries, including dancer and flamencologist Fernando Rodríguez Gómez, commonly known as Fernando de Triana, who noted that even though she was not of Gitana descent, she understood traditional flamenco and cante jondo and danced the "purest" flamenco style.[14]

La Argentinita received a formal dance education and began performing as a professional at the age of six. Early in her career she appeared in music halls alongside Pastora Imperio and also became famous for her innovative works and collaborations with members of the Generation of 1927. The most important of these were her recordings of classical Spanish songs with Lorca on the piano.[15] She is credited with raising flamenco to a high art by blending aspects of modernism with traditional cante jondo, and she adapted writings of the Generation of 1927 by using flamenco as the medium for theatrical dance dramas. One such work is the famous *El Café de Chinitas*, which is based on Lorca's poem and is still performed by flamenco companies today.[16] Like her contemporaries, La Argentinita believed in the preservation of popular and folkloric arts and incorporated them into modern theater. Her shows included everyday characters, and she used both local Gitano performers from the cafés cantantes and flamenco legends in her productions because she wanted to promote a style that was pure and true to the original form.

La Argentinita directed her own company and created six folklore-themed shows. In 1933 she premiered *Las Calles de Cádiz* (The Streets of Cadiz), and she produced her own version of *El Amor Brujo*, which emphasized folkloric and Gitano culture over classical dance. Based on another work by Lorca, *Las Calles de Cádiz* was one of the first productions to use flamencos, whose traditional style replaced classical Spanish dance. For her production of *El Café de Chinitas*, Salvador Dalí designed and created the set. In 1935, just before the onset of the Spanish Civil War, she went to New York and became an instant sensation. Staying in exile throughout the war, she gained the title of the first true "American flamenca." After a European tour, she returned to the United States in 1943 and never went back to Spain, passing away in New York in 1945.[17]

Spain's most prominent male dancer of this period was Vicente Escudero. His rise to fame was partially due to his discovery by La Argentina and their early collaborations. He was neither Gitano nor from Andalusia and spent most of his formative years in Paris among the avant-garde; he was considered Spain's first abstract modernist flamenco dancer. But rather than incorporating flamenco into modern theater, Escudero incorporated the lines and aesthetics of modern art into his technique and choreography. Inspired by the works of his personal friends the Spanish surrealist Joan Miró and Picasso, Escudero painted many dance images, imbuing them with a modernist aesthetic and his knowledge of dance technique. Still photos of his dance movements resemble the abstract and cubist paintings of the era.

The performing careers and projects of all these artists changed how we perceive flamenco. They also demonstrate that even for the professional and modern artist, Andalusia remains the cradle of flamenco, where the acolyte comes to study, live among the people, and be inspired by the Gitano way of life. The theatrical rise of flamenco in Madrid, Barcelona, Paris, and London spilled over to the Americas, including New York, Mexico City, Buenos Aires, and Havana. In the United States,

Encarnación López y Júlvez, "La Argentinita," 1922.
Photograph by Kurt Hielscher.

An image of La Argentinita from an early biography, *Libro de Confidencias* (Book of Secrets), c. 1913–1920.

flamenco's introduction took place on a large scale due to artists such as La Argentina, La Argentinita, and Vicente Escudero. But perhaps the most famous dancer outside Spain was Carmen Amaya, who was a young child during the great theatrical era. Born to a Gitano family in Barcelona, she lived and breathed the sights and sounds of flamenco in her home and in the theaters and *tablaos* (flamenco bars or clubs) of the day. She shot to stardom using a new brand of flamenco inspired by her personal history, style, and technique.

Pareja de Baile en Tonos Rojos (Dance Couple in Red Tones) by Vicente Escudero, c. 1948. Wax, pencil, paper. In addition to incorporating modernist aesthetics into his dance, Escudero also became an accomplished painter. He regarded his dance style as "architectural," which he illustrated in his paintings of solo dancers and couples.

opposite:
 Vicente Escudero, c. 1960s. Photographs by Colita. These images illustrate the modernist qualities of Escudero's dance. His poses are at once classic yet represent shapes and forms found in avant-garde art of the early to mid-twentieth century.

CIVIL WAR: END OF THE GOLDEN ERA

The abundance of artistic collaboration that took place throughout the 1920s and 1930s came to an abrupt end with the onset of the Spanish Civil War in 1936. For many artists, writers, and scholars in the flamenco community, the outbreak of the Spanish Civil War symbolized the end of the golden era. La Argentina died of cardiac arrest on the very day the war broke out, and Lorca was later executed by Franco's troops. Falla left in 1939 for Argentina, where he continued to have a prolific career until his death. Other artists and writers of the Generation of 1927 left Spain in voluntary exile and headed for the larger cities of the Americas, including Mexico City and Buenos Aires. The artists who left the country continued their careers overseas, bringing the traditions of flamenco and Spanish dance to new audiences, which led to the proliferation of flamenco in the United States and other countries.

Inside Spain, the cante jondo of the Gitanos went underground, only to emerge as a more sanitized version of flamenco. Artists who did not leave the country eventually performed and even starred in large touring companies, in films, and

Zambra de la Golondrina (Cave of the Swallow) in the Sacromonte neighborhood, Granada, Spain, c. 1950s. The caves of the Sacromonte have been handed down through generations of Gitano families, and this *zambra* was founded by the grandparents of José Valle Fajardo (Chuscales) in 1947. These establishments provided a space for families to continue their artistic traditions.

at public festivals sanctioned by the government. Performers often had to get past censors and adhere to strict government guidelines.[18]

In 1947, the Spanish Ministry of Culture and the Department of Tourism launched an advertising campaign known in English as "Spain Is Different." Although unofficial until 1957, it was put into action in the 1960s, advertising an exotic Spain of unique regional cultures. The result was a tourism boom unlike anything seen before.[19] Many artists who lived through the Spanish Civil War continued teaching and performing in establishments such as flamenco tablaos, *ventas* (roadside restaurants dedicated to showing flamenco), and the famous caves of the Sacromonte district of Granada—all of which provided entertainment for the growing tourist population. *España de la pandereta*, or Spain of the tambourine (a term used to describe the romanticized image of the country), was alive and well. Spain had become the land of sun, beaches, bullfights, flamenco, and sherry.

Several decades after flamenco was first introduced to the United States, students and aficionados alike traveled to Spain to learn and study. From the survivors and descendants of the bygone golden era, these new students learned the art of flamenco.

Chapter 2

Flamenco in the United States

Flamenco and Spanish dance reached a pinnacle in the United States at the end of the nineteenth century. The "Spanish craze" was a period during which all things Spanish, including literature, art, music, architecture, and fashion, were in vogue among wealthier Americans. Lasting from the 1880s until the end of the 1920s, the craze reached its height immediately after the Spanish-American War in 1898, and some aspects of it continued well into the 1940s and 1950s. It began among the educated elite in university departments of Spanish language and literature and then spread to art collectors and music aficionados.[1] A simultaneous rise of the upper middle class led to increased foreign travel in search of the picturesque and the "other." Spain provided the perfect combination of the exotic and the comforts of home.[2]

CROSSING THE ATLANTIC

Although the Spanish craze included dance and music, earlier factors contributed to the rise in popularity of flamenco and Spanish dance. The first was the arrival of the Austrian dancer Fanny Elssler. Born Franziska Elssler in Gumpendorf, Vienna, she came from a musical family; her father worked as a copyist for Austrian composer Franz Joseph Haydn. Elssler, who was credited as being one of the greatest ballet dancers of the romantic era, incorporated traditional folk dances into ballet. In her performance in the Spanish dance *la cachucha*, she wore a Florinda costume of pink satin trimmed with black lace, which was copied by many

Program for Carmen Amaya performance, c. 1950s.

Carmencita by William Merritt Chase, 1890.
Oil on canvas, 69 7⁄8 x 40 7⁄8 in.

Viennese women. Elssler first appeared in the United States in 1840 at the Park Theater in New York and then toured the eastern states, including a special performance for President Martin Van Buren, who was a former musician. Popular lore holds that Congress was suspended, legislators carried her through the streets, and fans drank champagne from her slippers. Her earnings were so prodigious that she broke her contract with the Paris Opera to extend her North American tour for nearly three years to 1842.[3]

Throughout the second half of the nineteenth century, with a dramatic increase after the American Civil War, Spanish dancers continued to arrive, performing in vaudeville venues and dance halls. Most performed the escuela bolera, which was the rage among audiences hungry for the bohemian lifestyle.[4] The first dancer of the flamenco genre was Trinidad Huertas, "La Cuenca," who arrived in 1888. A star of the Andalusian cafés cantantes, she was one of the few women, along with her partner the Gitana dancer Juana la Macarrona, to leave Spain and travel abroad. Huertas broke the stereotype of an enticing woman bedecked in ruffles by wearing the *traje de luces* (suit of lights) costume of a Spanish bullfighter.

In 1890 Spanish dancer Carmen Dauset Moreno, "Carmencita," arrived in New York, and she had her first public performance two years later in Boston's Chickering Hall. Known as the "Pearl of Seville," she became a star and an honored member of New York's intellectual elite; her friendships included the painters Joaquín Sorolla and William Merritt Chase, for whom she did a private performance in his studio. Carmencita's brother-in-law Antonio Grau Mora, "El Rojo el Alpargatero" (Antonio the Red Shoemaker), accompanied her to New York and sang for her performances; he may have been the first male flamenco singer in New York.[5] In 1894 Thomas Edison recorded Carmencita's movements in a film that is preserved in the Library of Congress. The footage not only attests to her talent but to the importance of dance in the minds of early videographers.

The First World War and the postwar period, often referred to as the Roaring Twenties or the Jazz Age, saw a marked increase in migrants leaving Europe in search of a better life in the United States. There was an influx of writers, actors, artists, dancers, musicians, and poets. In 1916 Spanish composer Enrique Granados arrived in New York to work on a production of his *Goyescas* (1915), and he invited the well-known Spanish dancer and choreographer La Argentina to choreograph and star in it. Often referred to as the "Spanish Pavlova," her arrival in New York prompted a surge in the popularity of Spanish dance. Although the theater director turned La Argentina's job over to another dancer, Granados composed a special piece in her honor titled *La Danza de los Ojos Verdes* (The Dance of the Green Eyes). La Argentina performed along the East Coast, in Detroit, and then in Puerto Rico, Cuba, Venezuela, and Mexico, returning to the United States via Texas. Back in New York she starred in 1917–1918 in a Spanish-American production of *The Land of Joy* by Joaquín Valverde Sanjuán, for which she received complimentary reviews in the *New York Times*. In 1920, she once again toured Mexico, Cuba,

This is one of the few motion shots that exist of La Argentina.
She is rehearsing her dance *Sevillana* at the Town Hall theater
in New York, 1935. Photograph by R. M. Anderson.

and Texas, then returned in 1928 for performances at New York's Town Hall and
Carnegie Hall, which were followed by performances in Boston, Chicago, Detroit,
Philadelphia, and Toronto.[6]

In 1929 La Argentina traveled to the West Coast, then toured Honolulu, Tokyo,
Hong Kong, Shanghai, Singapore, and Manila. In December of that year, Lorca,
who had arrived in New York in 1925, organized a special *homenaje* (homage or tribute) for her at Columbia University.[7] In 1932 and 1933 she toured both North and
South America, presenting her version of Falla's *El Amor Brujo* at the world-famous

Teatro Colón in Buenos Aires. In 1935, a year before her death, she was invited back to the United States for a special performance at the White House, which was followed by more performances in New York.

La Argentina's flamenco was engraved in the minds of the millions who were fortunate enough to see her. She brought to the United States her own version of theatrical Spanish dance, imbued with her classical training and inspired by the Gitanos of southern Spain.[8] She also introduced new performers to the United States, including dancer Vicente Escudero, who arrived in 1931. Escudero was originally invited to dance with Anna Pavlova, but the tour was cut short because of her untimely death. After performing with La Argentina, he starred in his own shows, which were produced by impresario Sol Hurok. Escudero was the first male flamenco to gain recognition in the United States, and he inspired generations of men to study and become dancers. He was unique, artistic, modern, and experimental while remaining true to flamenco's essence. In 1934 he was invited by Falla to perform in *El Amor Brujo*, which opened at the San Francisco Opera House and traveled to theaters throughout the United States. New York critics wrote that Escudero's success was remarkable for the time. Even though he did not tour outside Spain as often as La Argentina did (his last international tour was in 1955–1956), Escudero left a memorable American legacy before returning to France and Spain, where he spent most of his professional career. Expressing his love of flamenco through dance, painting, and film, he created a significant body of work that is displayed in museums and made movies that spread flamenco to a wide audience.[9]

As studios incorporated ethnic and folkloric dance into their repertoires during the 1940s–1950s, touring dance companies from Spain came to the United States. Job shortages during the Spanish Civil War and the period immediately after had resulted in an especially large influx of Spanish dancers, who were paid by nightclub owners, Broadway producers, and large resort hotels for extended stays. The Spanish craze had moved out of art galleries and literary circles into ballrooms, dance halls, theaters, and cinema. American students were inspired by the greatest performers of the theatrical era and experienced Spanish dance and flamenco firsthand.

Following her contemporaries La Argentina and Escudero, La Argentinita had arrived in New York in 1935. Already famous for her collaborations with Lorca and the Generation of 1927, she was known as the first populist/avant-garde flamenca. She enjoyed ten prolific years in New York and throughout the United States, presenting a variety of theatrical pieces, including *El Romance de los Peregrinos* (The Romance of the Pilgrims), *Ávila, Madrid 1890*, and *La Romería de los Cornudos* (The Pilgrimage of the Cuckolds). She traveled back to her home country only briefly, and in 1943, after an extended European tour, returned to the United States with plans to stay, premiering her newest version of *El Café de Chinitas* at the Metropolitan Opera House. It was a collaborative masterpiece originally written by Lorca, with set designs by Salvador Dalí. For the New York debut, Basque musician

Argentinita Dance Album: Twelve Selected Dances and Songs from Her Repertoire, 1943. Cover and page for "Los Cuatro Muleros." Dance and music books were used by students throughout the United States to learn various Spanish dances, including classical, regional, and flamenco. This album contained sheet music, lyrics, and images of La Argentinita in costume.

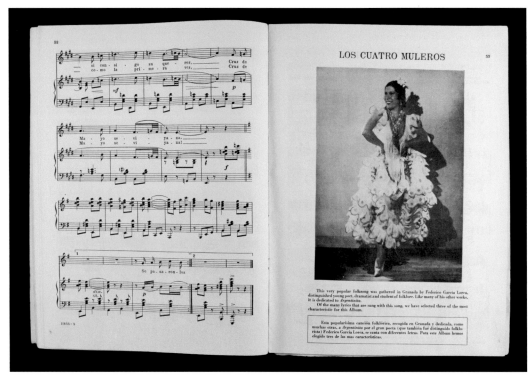

Castanets, Spain, c. 1940–1950. These castanets belonged to La
Argentinita and have been handed down to other dancers over
the years.

José Iturbi conducted the orchestra. The show gained an international following
surpassing all others up to that time.[10] La Argentinita remained in New York until
her untimely death at the age of forty-seven.

La Argentinita and her sister Pilar López worked closely together, with Pilar
performing in many of La Argentinita's productions. After La Argentinita's death,
López remained in New York, continuing to direct the company and carrying
forward the spirit and tradition of her sister. In 1949 López commissioned a statue
of La Argentinita by sculptor Rosario Murabito. The piece was dedicated at the old
Metropolitan Opera House and is permanently housed in the Opera Guild room.[11]
López eventually returned to Spain to direct her own company. She enjoyed a prolific career of more than thirty years, touring her company of flamenco and Spanish
dancers around the world. She performed into her late seventies. In the tradition
of her sister, she was the first to hire several American dancers who later became
stars, including José Greco (Brooklyn), Teo Morca (Los Angeles), Pablo Rodarte
(Denver), and Vicente Romero (Santa Fe). Several of these flamencos later created
their own companies, toured the United States, and inspired future professional
and amateur dancers along the way.

Pilar López was known not only for her classic style but also for searching out the most talented male dancers and introducing them to audiences around the world. Here, she is pictured with dancers Alejandro de la Vega and Paco de Alba in Madrid, Spain, 1964. Photograph by Colita.

La Argentinita and Pilar López created a fervor for Spanish dance that outlasted the golden era of dance in their home country. Throughout the 1930s–1950s, many touring companies followed their lead and enjoyed great success in the United States. The dynamic duo of Florence Pérez Padilla and Antonio Ruiz Soler, popularly known as Rosario and Antonio, or Los Chavalillos Sevillanos (The Young Kids from Seville), enjoyed twenty years of touring and starred in two Hollywood movies. They were so well received that during their tenure not a single issue of *Dance Magazine* was printed without some mention of them. When their partnership finally broke up, Antonio formed a troupe called Antonio and His Spanish Dancers; they were considered among the greatest Spanish dancers in the world.

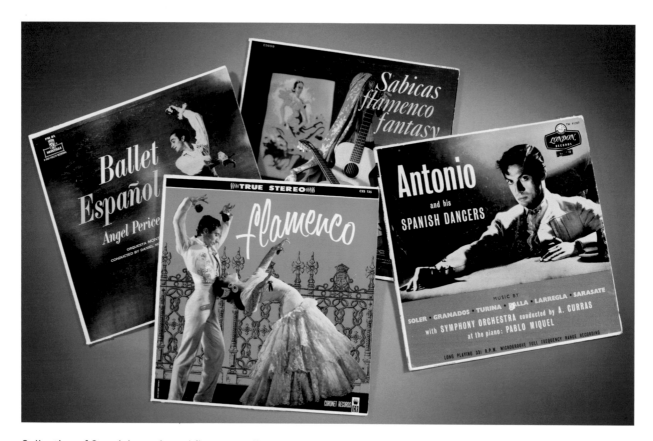

Collection of Spanish music and flamenco albums, c. 1950s. During the 1950s, Spanish rhythms and melodies filtered into popular music. Albums such as these were often the first introduction to the various genres of Spanish music, since young dancers often did not have the opportunity to dance to live music.

As dancers gained experience, many started their own companies, including Pilar López, Roberto Ximenez and Manolo Vargas (who joined forces), Antonio, and Carmen Amaya.[12] Amaya's brand of passionate flamenco profoundly impacted American audiences. Of pure Gitano blood, she arrived on the American scene with a reputation established in Spain and South America for virtuosity, rapid-fire footwork, and wearing pants. She was raised in Somorrostro, an impoverished Gitano barrio in Barcelona, and was encouraged by her father to begin dancing in nightclubs at age five.[13] By age seven, she was dancing in a show headlined by Raquel Meller, one of the great *cancionistas* (singers of Spanish popular songs) of the era. Amaya left Spain during the civil war, taking her entire entourage of nearly forty family and company members with her. They toured throughout Mexico and South America, where Amaya's success allowed her to buy a home in Buenos Aires. Word of her incredible talent drew impresario Sol Hurok to Buenos Aires.

Carmen Amaya, c. 1945.

opposite:
Carmen Amaya depicted in her signature pantsuit, c. 1950s.

He offered Amaya's company a five-year contract and convinced her to come to the United States.

Amaya's New York debut took place at the Beachcomber in 1941, which was followed by a stop in Hollywood to film her first movie, *Panama Hattie* (1942); she appeared in a dance scene but was uncredited. She became the doyenne of Spanish dance and the epitome of pure, raw, untamable Gypsy flamenco, with fans and

Carmen Amaya, Begur, Girona, Spain, 1963. Photograph by
Colita. This image is one of the last taken before her death, at
an old farmhouse she bought to use for *concursos* and festivals.

aficionados flocking to theaters to see her.[14] Although she enjoyed a great run in
New York, it was the West Coast that called to Amaya and her family members,
many of whom remained there even after she returned to Spain. In California and
Mexico, members of the Amaya clan passed on their traditions to budding guitar
students, singers, and dancers. Amaya eventually moved back to Begur, near Barce-

lona, where she bought and renovated an old barn and created an annual flamenco festival that is still held to this day.[15] She died of kidney failure in 1963, just before the release of her last film, *Los Tarantos*.

WESTWARD MIGRATION

The influence of Spanish and Latin American styles continued to spread to architecture, interior design, arts and crafts, and fashion. No longer a fad enjoyed only by elite society in larger cities, Spanish and Latin American performances took place in a multitude of dance halls, nightclubs, and smaller venues. Spanish immigrants also spread the traditional folkloric and regional dances from their homeland, and several early schools of Spanish dance and dance companies developed in the mid-twentieth century in the American West.

The introduction of Spanish dance coincided with a wider revival of folk, ethnic, and traditional arts. Rising industrialism and urban growth, spurred on by technological innovations, were leading to a loss of cultural heritage, which was counteracted by preservationist movements that began with arts and crafts and then spread to the stages and theaters of Europe and the Americas. The Ballets Russes, for example, transformed ballet into a modern mix of classical dance and tribal rhythms, movements, and costumes. Composers and playwrights such as Falla and Lorca incorporated Gitano heritage and traditions into modern theatrical productions. Dance studios, which traditionally taught ballet, tap, and sometimes jazz, incorporated into their repertoires regional and folkloric dances from all over the world, including Spain.

In 1915, Ted Shawn and Ruth St. Denis had founded the Denishawn School of Dancing and Related Arts in Los Angeles. Like many modern dancers and artists of the era, they were inspired by folk traditions, Spanish dance, and the Ballets Russes. The company produced several Spanish- and Gitano-inspired productions, the first of which was a 1922 collaboration between Ted Shawn and modern dancer Martha Graham titled *La Malagueña*. In 1923 the company presented *Cuadro Flamenco*. Even though it was not staged in the traditional cuadro (group) format with the performers sitting in a semicircle accompanied by live singing and guitars, this theatrical presentation echoed Shawn's experiences in Spain and was informed by his knowledge of the famous dance masters of the era.[16] During the 1930s, after he and St. Denis had separated, Shawn began the Jacob's Pillow dance workshops in Becket, Massachusetts, initiating one of the oldest dance festivals in the United States concentrating on jazz, modern dance, and ballet. Flamenco was eventually incorporated into the offerings.[17]

Flamenco was also spread through schools founded by Spanish immigrants, including the Cansino family. Originally vaudeville actors, the brothers Eduardo and José Cansino settled in Los Angeles, where they opened a studio, and their sister Elisa Cansino had a studio in San Francisco. The Cansinos were the first

teachers of several artists who would pursue professional careers in Spain and the United States. Several of these professionals eventually ended up in New Mexico, while others left New Mexico to learn Spanish dance with the Cansinos.

Originally an aspiring auto mechanic in Los Angeles, Teo Morca took a class in music appreciation and was given a homework assignment to attend a classical concert. Accidentally, he stumbled into the wrong theater and ended up seeing Ana María and her Ballet Español at the Philharmonic Auditorium in Los Angeles. The concert changed his life. He continued working at the auto shop but took dance classes in the Hollywood studio of Ruth St. Denis (who had opened her own studio after the breakup of her marriage to Shawn and of the Denishawn company), which were followed by classes with the Cansino family. Morca performed with José Cansino's group, where he starred in a major dance recital, and he soon decided to pursue a full-time dance career.[18]

In a similar story, Lydia Torea from Phoenix, Arizona, started dance lessons (ballet, jazz, and tap) early in life. Of half-Polish, half-Spanish descent, she was eager to meet other Spanish immigrant families in the community and tagged along with her mother and grandmother to Spanish Club meetings in the basement of a church. At one of these events she met Eddie Fernández, a local Spanish dance instructor, who was born in Asturias in northern Spain and had studied with José Cansino. Like many students, Torea did not study flamenco right away but instead learned a range of Spanish dances, including folk dances such as the jota and the popular paso doble.[19]

opposite, left:
Teo Morca at age seventeen, with guitarist Geronimo Villarino at the studio of Eduardo Cansino, c. 1951.

opposite, right:
Morca was the second American dancer to be chosen by Pilar López to be a lead performer in her company. Here, they are pictured together on stage in 1967.

Lydia Torea as a young student with teacher Eddie Fernández in a photo used for his Christmas card in 1950.

Before Morca's and Torea's introduction to Spanish dance, native Santa Fean Betty Serna Cárdenas had experienced regional, folkloric, and traditional Spanish and Mexican dances at community gatherings and celebrations in Santa Fe and Northern New Mexico. During the 1940s, she studied dance at La Gitana Dance Studio on the corner of Canyon Road and Delgado Street. Although Cárdenas's focus was tap and ballet, her teacher introduced her to Hungarian folk dancing and classical Spanish dance. After graduating from high school in 1947, Cárdenas moved to California to continue her dance studies at the San Francisco Ballet School, and there she heard about a teacher giving Spanish dance lessons. The teacher was none other than Elisa Cansino, and Cárdenas studied with her in San Francisco. This early education inspired further study and a career as a Spanish dancer upon Cárdenas's return to New Mexico in 1949.[20]

Christmas postcard featuring the hands of Spanish dancer Elisa Cansino playing the castanets, San Francisco, c. 1949–1950.

A young Betty Serna Cárdenas before a performance in San Francisco, c. 1948–1949.

JOSÉ GRECO: BROOKLYN PHENOMENON

Traveling companies headed by dance legends inspired many studios to incorporate classical Spanish dances and flamenco into their repertoires. Even so, opportunities for a non-Spaniard to dance as a professional in the Spanish genre were rare. That would change when a young American boy from Brooklyn became one of the world's most renowned Spanish dancers.

José Greco was born Montorio dei Frentani, Italy, in 1918. When he was ten, his family came to the United States and settled in Brooklyn, where they lived among other Italian immigrant families. During his teens Greco was an aspiring art student at the Leonardo da Vinci Art School in New York. Drawing and painting the human figure was his favorite subject, and he often frequented dance shows for inspiration. At a performance by the great master Vicente Escudero, Greco decided then and there to pursue a career in dance.[21]

Greco attended dance classes at the studio of Helen Viola, along with his sister Lorinda, who later became an opera singer with the Metropolitan Opera. Although he only had two years of formal training, he made his professional debut in the opera *Carmen* in 1937 at New York's Hippodrome. The following year he returned in a production of *La Traviata* and then began performing at New York nightclubs and teaching "everything from the samba to the Suzie Q" at hotels and resorts.[22] His nightclub act at Manhattan's La Conga was noticed in 1942 by La Argentinita, who asked him to join her company. After his first performance with her at Carnegie Hall, he shot to stardom and was given featured billing and solo numbers. He also became La Argentinita's official onstage partner.[23] A few years after his first appearance with her, *Dance Magazine* raved about his talent:

> The name José Greco is a comparatively new one in the dance world—but it is a name to watch. . . . The handsome young man to whom it belongs came out of nowhere, it seemed, only a few years ago, and is now flashing across the horizons of dance like a brilliant and exciting meteor. Partner to Argentinita, and premier danseur of her famous troupe, he has been acclaimed by critics throughout the land for his flawless technique and inspired interpretations of difficult Spanish dance forms. . . . Greco is to the dance world what Frank Sinatra is to popular music.[24]

Greco remained La Argentinita's leading man until her death in 1945. He then partnered with Pilar López and toured as her leading man for three years. He eventually formed his own company of Spanish dancers, which debuted to rave reviews in Spain, where he was proclaimed a bona fide Spaniard even though he was of Italian heritage and from Brooklyn. His company toured Europe and appeared in England at the Sadler's Wells Theatre in 1951. Shortly thereafter, the company returned to the United States, where it was a huge success, touring the North American continent for several years. In 1959, shortly after Greco's second visit to

London, the British magazine *Dance and Dancers* described him as "still under the influence of Spain and of the López sisters. He had an arresting appearance with his finely chiseled features, splendid physique and great power in the lower half of his body." The article went on to state that his style was imbued with "typical characteristics of American showmanship" and added that there was no doubt Greco could "put on a show."[25]

Indeed, Greco could put on a show, and his company was one of the most renowned in the dance world. In 1953 he broke attendance records at the Hollywood Bowl with an audience of 18,500. The *Los Angeles Examiner*'s reviewer

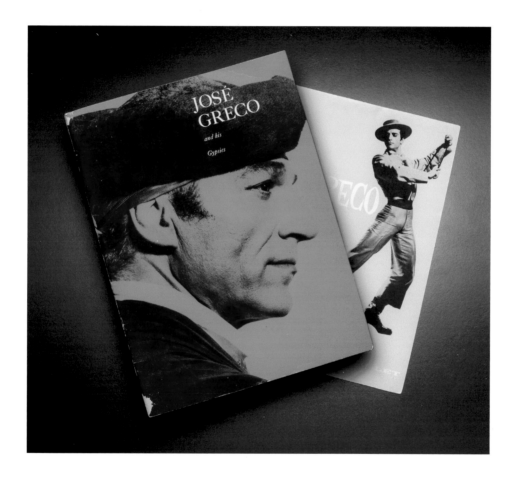

Playbills for José Greco and His Spanish Ballet, c. 1950s.
Greco's looks and style embodied the ideal male stereotype for
Spanish and flamenco dance.

opposte:
José Greco demonstrates his classic acrobatic leaps and
dynamic moves, c. 1950s.

Lydia Torea dancing alongside José Greco in the film *Ship of Fools*, 1965.

stated that the "audience all but filled the Bowl, hundreds were still streaming in at intermission time and for all I know they may still be streaming in as you read this." The journalist also reported, "Greco was in his customary immaculate form, his heel and toe work had the rapidity of riveting machines and he used the techniques of the Spanish Dancer for both comedy and drama."[26] Surpassing Carmen Amaya's top audience of 18,000 and matching the size of her fan club, Greco and his company toured the United States and throughout the world for more than four decades and received rave reviews wherever they went. In 1963, having danced for nearly twenty-five years, he was described as "ageless and beyond change: he dances as well, if not better, every year."[27]

Greco scoured Spain and the United States for fresh, up-and-coming talent, as well as for the top tier of experienced dancers, singers, and musicians for his company. Performers from Spain who appeared in his company included dancer Matilde Coral and guitarist Paco de Lucía. David Briggs, a guitarist and Spanish professor, recalled that Greco's talents included both his expertise as a great dancer and his ability to discover some of the greatest flamenco performers in the world.[28]

Greco inspired and launched the careers of many young dancers in the United States. Members of his company learned from performing in his shows and from life on the road with Spaniards and Gitanos, who handed down the flamenco tradition at after-show gatherings, meals, and celebrations. It was in such a setting that Lydia Torea met a young Paco de Lucía while she was preparing a meal for company members in her hotel room.[29] One newspaper article claimed that Greco had "his eye on every young person who ever donned the flamenco boots and fingered castanets between Phoenix, Arizona, and Madrid, Spain."[30] Greco himself stated that he enjoyed looking for talented individuals in the Southwest because "New Mexico and that area of the States has retained a pure Spanish tradition, purer even than Mexico."[31] Greco saw Torea for the first time in Phoenix, and when he later met her again in Spain, he hired her on the spot. Beginning at the age of nineteen, she toured with the company for three years between 1962 and 1965, starring as one of Greco's leading ladies. She also appeared with him in the film *Ship of Fools*, which was nominated for an Academy Award for best picture in 1965. Later, several people who performed with Greco, including Morca, Torea, and Vicente Romero, would influence the flamenco scene in New Mexico.

MOTION PICTURES: FLAMENCO FOR THE MASSES

Greco appeared on *The Dinah Shore Chevy Show* at least three times between 1958 and 1959. He enjoyed roles in five major films: *Sombrero* (1953), *Around the World in Eighty Days* (1956), *Holiday for Lovers* (1959), *Ship of Fools* (1965), and *The Proud and Damned* (1972). Spanish dance and music, even if only featured in one memorable segment, was thus conveyed to a broader audience than ever before. Although concert halls and theaters were important venues, films were viewed by the masses.

The earliest film that included Spanish dance was produced in 1894 by Thomas Edison and featured dancer Carmencita. Edison's movie pre-dated the "official" invention of cinema by the Lumière brothers, who made their first movie in 1896. The Lumière brothers debuted their own early film of Spanish dancers in 1900 at the Parisian Exposition Universelle.[32]

The 1920s saw the advent of the Latin lover as personified by actor Rudolph Valentino. Epitomizing the romantic paradigm of the Spanish craze, Valentino mixed the imagery of various Latin cultures, including flamenco, the Argentine tango, and the costuming of an Argentine gaucho. This merging of Latino and

Hispano imagery continued after the decline of the Spanish craze and reached new-found popularity in the post–World War II era and the affluent 1950s.

In 1941, actress Rita Hayworth, who was a member of the Cansino family, showed off her singing and dancing talents in a remake of the 1922 classic film *Blood and Sand*, which had starred Valentino. The film is filled with the imagery and themes of *España de la pandereta*, including a story of love and betrayal when a bullfighter is lured away from his wife by the haunting songs of an enticing woman. Despite the stereotypes, the inclusion of Hayworth, a Spaniard who knew the dance, music, and customs of Spain, made a huge impact on the quality of the film and brought Spanish culture to the forefront of Hollywood cinema.

Some Hollywood films featured dancers and musicians who portrayed themselves. This genre includes two films starring the dance duo Rosario and Antonio: *Ziegfeld Girl* (1941) and *Hollywood Canteen* (1944). Carmen Amaya starred in seventeen motion pictures made in Hollywood, Spain, and Latin America. Her last, *Los Tarantos*, was nominated for an Academy Award.

Movies such as *Los Tarantos* and *Sombrero* brought Spanish dance and music to audiences across the United States, including those in remote locations where traveling companies had little or no presence. These films reached thousands of prospective fans, aficionados, future students, and aspiring professionals. In 1953 Greco's appearance in the movie *Sombrero* inspired at least one young boy from Santa Fe, New Mexico, to become a Spanish dancer. But even before the touring companies and cinema performances, this corner of the Southwest was no stranger to Spanish music and dance. New Mexico and other parts of the greater Southwest had known centuries of Spanish and Hispano culture, including traditional songs, folkloric dances, pageants, and plays performed on town plazas and city streets. These cultural traditions would soon include flamenco as part of New Mexico's Spanish heritage.

opposite:
Stills from Carmen Amaya's last film, *Los Tarantos*, 1963.
Photographs by Colita.

Chapter 3

Feria and Fiesta Traditions in Spain and New Mexico

Throughout all of the changes and advances discussed in the previous chapters, and even during the Spanish Civil War, traditional flamenco survived in the homes and public festivals of Andalusian pueblos and villages. Ingrained in the people of southern Spain for centuries, flamenco had traveled to other regions of the country by the beginning of the twentieth century, and there were pockets of Gitano and flamenco families in larger cities such as Barcelona and Madrid. Music, song, and dance were intrinsic to family life, and local and regional forms continued to be passed down from generation to generation. Young artists made their debuts via regional *concursos* (competitions) and local festivals and *ferias* (fairs).

SPRING IN SPAIN: FERIAS AND THE FLAMENCO SPIRIT

The most renowned outburst of flamenco in Spain is during *ferias de primavera*. In these spring fairs, young and old, rich and poor, city dwellers and villagers alike gather to celebrate the end of Lent, Semana Santa (Holy Week), the beginning of spring, and the eventual coming of summer. Festivals and fairs are held all over Spain, each imbued with its own regional character. In the south, the feria reflects the flamenco spirit.

The largest of all these celebrations is Seville's Feria de Abril (April Fair). Beginning exactly two weeks after the end of Semana Santa, it kicks off the spring season for the rest of the region. Every week thereafter each city, town, and village

Fairgoers in Seville, Spain, 2012. Photograph by author.

Couple on horseback, Seville, Spain, c. 1960s. The man is dressed in the classic *traje campero* (or *traje corto*), while the woman wears a *traje de gitana* and sits sidesaddle.

Woman holding child, Seville, Spain, c. 1960s. *Feria* costumes were worn by all members of the family.

celebrates its own unique feria. For example, in Jerez the Fiesta del Caballo (Festival of the Horse) recognizes the city's Andalusian breeds and the local Real Escuela Andaluza del Arte Equestre (Royal School of Andalusian Equestrian Arts). The fair in nearby Sanlúcar de Barrameda is known as the Feria de Manzanilla, referring to a sherry for which the city is famous. Ferias generally last for an entire week in larger towns and for three- or four-day extended weekends in smaller towns. An avid fairgoer can spend almost two months attending ferias in a variety of towns.

The April Fair in Seville began as a *feria de ganado*, an agrarian and livestock trade fair. The event dates back to 1254 CE under King Alfonso X, who also happened to be a great lover and promoter of music and dance. Ranchers and farm families brought their stock to a designated area near the outskirts of town. Once the business activities were finished, evening festivities and celebrations with food, drink, music, and dancing commenced, frequently going all night. The lower and

Posters for spring festivities in Seville, Spain, 1904 and 1943. Posters such as these advertised Semana Santa (Holy Week), the April Fair, and the opening of the spring bullfighting season.

Children's *feria* dresses, Seville, Spain, 1990s (*left*) and 1960s
(*right*). Cotton, satin ribbon.

opposite:
Traje de gitana (*feria* dress), c. 1940s. Cotton, satin ribbon.

Father and children on horseback, Seville, Spain, 2012. Photograph by author.

Traje campero (countryman's suit), Madrid, Spain, c. 1970s.

middle classes often dressed *de gitana*, in clothing typical of Gitanos, while the wealthy wore their finest, trendy Parisian fashions. The typical costume for a young woman dressed de gitana was a *traje de volantes* (ruffled dress), often with a bustle and train. Covered in polka dots, the preferred pattern of Gitanas, these dresses celebrated the season in a multitude of vibrant spring colors. Bracelets and earrings made of carved wood and painted in bright colors completed the outfit. The *traje campero* (countryman's suit) was reserved for men on horseback.[1] The feria grounds were like a miniature city, including streets lined with tented structures of white canvas, referred to as *casetas*. These "homes away from home" were places of hospitality where family and friends enjoyed sherry, tapas, live music, and dancing until sunrise. During the sunny afternoons, wealthy landowners paraded their horse-drawn carriages down the streets, showing off their finest equine breeds.

The first spring fair in Seville organized by the city took place on April 18, 19, and 20, 1846. The autumn fair, which began in 1875, was referred to as the Feria de San Miguel. It was held on the feast day of St. Michael and corresponded with the autumnal equinox. Spearheading the creation and planning of the earliest ferias were two men, a Basque resident named José María Ybarra and a *catalán* named Narciso Bonaplata. Both were businessmen and members of Seville's municipal corporation. According to accounts by Ybarra, the first event had nineteen casetas and 25,000 people in attendance. For the evening festivities, vendors sold wine from Valdepeñas and the mountain towns of Los Arados and La Fonda and brandy from Cazalla de la Sierra. The food included chorizo, menudo, fried fish, *migas* (a bread and meat mixture), and *caldereta* (a combination of rice and seafood or meat, baked in a casserole dish). Ybarra and Bonaplata believed the feria would be a solution to the city's economic crisis, and they were not disappointed. The first feria brought in 400,000 duros in one week.[2]

Seville's April Fair originally took place at the Prado de Sebastián, an area outside of town. It later moved to the Parque de María Luisa, a lush public park that also served as the grounds for the Ibero-American Exposition of 1929. Seville's fair ran annually until the Spanish Civil War (1936–1939) and resumed in 1940. During the postwar period, all fairs and festivals underwent a period of *tipísmo* (a refinement of character and style), which refers to the incorporation of regional differences and stereotypical styles. This was prompted in part by Prime Minister Francisco Franco's push to increase tourism through his Spain Is Different campaign. Portraying Spain as a unified country of unique regional cultures and traditions, the campaign began in 1947 but was not fully in place until the 1960s. At that time, the promotion of Spain's regional festivals took place on a grand scale, and Seville's April Fair became a major tourist attraction, drawing luminaries such as Grace Kelly and Jacqueline Kennedy Onassis. Another campaign, Festivales de España, was initiated by the Ministry of Culture during the 1950s and 1960s, and it provided funds for the presentation of regional dance and music by large performance companies, such as Pilar López and her Ballet Español. Throughout the country, government-

Fiesta en una Caseta de Feria by Manuel Cabral Bejarano, 1860.
Oil on linen, 19 7/10 x 25 6/10 in. This painting illustrates the interior
of a tent where friends and family have gathered for an all-night
party and celebration.

selected dancers and musicians followed the festival circuit, presenting an array of
popular Spanish dances, including folkloric, classical, escuela bolera, and flamenco.
Only in the south were there concerts solely devoted to flamenco.[3]

Andalusian fairs grew immensely during this time period, taking on the forms
we still enjoy today. In 1949 a *portada* (gate) was first added to the Seville April
Fair, and it is now a major component of the annual tradition. The portada is the
grand entryway into the fairgrounds, and lighting the gate marks the beginning of
the week, while turning off the lights marks the finale, which is accompanied by
fireworks and further merriment. The official end of a feria, however, does not take
place until all fairgoers are at home in their beds.

Casetas are a major component of ferias. The first gas lamps were installed in
casetas and along the streets in 1866, which was followed three years later by a gas
distribution system. In 1885 the main thoroughfare, Calle San Fernando, was lined
with gas lanterns that illuminated the night skies. In the late nineteenth century,
casetas had ornate exteriors and decorative interior designs tailored to look like tav-
erns or elegant salons. Eventually families or groups of friends gave names to their
casetas, making them easier to find. Wealthier families hired musicians, singers, and

Portada (entrance gate) to the Feria de Abril (April Fair), Seville, Spain, 2012.
Photograph by author.

Furniture for the interior of a *caseta de feria* by Muebles Ávila, Seville, Spain, 2012. Shown is the classic style made by hand throughout Andalusia.

Fairgoers in Seville, Spain, 2012. Photograph by author.

dancers for special performances. King Alfonso XIII and Queen Victoria Eugenie visited a caseta in 1913 and again in 1916. During the latter visit, they saw a performance by cantaora Rocío Vega, "La Niña de la Alfalfa," in the caseta of the workers union.

In 1973 the Seville April Fair moved to its more spacious current location on the outskirts of the Los Remedios neighborhood across the Guadalquivir River from the city center. Aside from the all-night dancing and entertainment, another major attraction is the parade of horses that takes place every afternoon. Landholding families dressed in their finest Gitano-style attire parade their Andalusian horses through the streets of the fairgrounds. The horses are bedecked in the traditional finery of the region, including *cascabeles* (bells) and *madroños* (wool or silk pompons on the headpiece). The cascabeles create a festive sound, much like winter sleigh bells, announcing the arrival of the horse-drawn carriages and the riders.

Feria outfits have become so important that there are now annual design competitions and runway shows featuring fiesta and flamenco costumes. The Salón Internacional de Moda Flamenca (SIMOF; International Salon of Flamenco Fashion), founded in 1994 by a cooperative of fashion designers, is dedicated to

Horse-drawn carriages parade the fairgrounds from late afternoon until sunset during the Fiesta del Caballo, Seville, Spain, 2012. Photograph by author.

Roberto Quijandria dresses Dorado de Domeq in the traditional horse gear for carriage. These are used solely for the parade of horses during fairs held in many cities of Andalusia. This set was made by Vicente Gonzales, Seville, Spain, 2013. Wool, leather, metal. Shot on location at Estancia Alegre, Alcalde, New Mexico, November 19, 2014.

Alexina García Chávez rides side saddle on top of Poesía in the manner of the April Fair. Shot on location at Estancia Alegre, Alcalde, New Mexico, December 16, 2014.

opposite:
Feria dress by Remedios Ramos Pérez, Seville, Spain, 2011. Cotton, lace, rayon.

creating contemporary trajes de volantes.[4] These dresses are "fashion for fashion's sake" and are typically more elaborate than stage costumes, which are lighter and easier to maneuver on stage. Wealthy fairgoers commission gifted designers to create them. Contrary to the stereotypical black-and-red costume of the flamenco dancer, the costumes of the feria tend to use bright, spring-like colors, with pale blues, lime greens, and oranges favored. Each year certain colors and styles dominate, and just like department stores begin stocking shelves for the holiday season, stores in Andalusia set up a seasonal section dedicated to all things feria. Elaborate

Accoutrements for a *feria* ensemble: *peine* (hair comb), *flor* (flower), *pendientes* (earrings), *abanico* (fan), Seville, Spain, 2008. Cotton, wood, plastic, metal.

opposite:
Contemporary *feria* dress with *mantoncito* (small shawl) by Hermanas Peregrino (Susana and Marta Pérez), Seville, Spain, 2008. Cotton, rayon.

retail displays re-create a caseta-like atmosphere, including a variety of sherries, and seasonal music, usually the *sevillanas*, is piped through a speaker system. In the streets, groups of people sing and clap their hands en route to the feria.

The sevillanas originated as a folkloric dance in which two people are partnered opposite each other. The song, dance, and music constitute one of the folkloric forms now adopted into the larger family of flamenco. Similar to the playing of holiday music in the United States for the entire month of December, the sevillanas can be heard in supermarkets, from automobile stereos, and sung by partiers in the streets. While sevillanas are considered the official music of the feria season, some towns choose local or regional tunes. In Jerez, for example, traditional flamenco/Gitano *bulerías* with fast, festive rhythm are preferred.

NEW MEXICO: FIESTA DE SANTA FE

Ferias and fiestas provide public spaces where Spanish people celebrate, share, show off, and rejoice in their traditional cultural heritage amid growing industrialism and globalization. The same holds true for the popular fiestas held throughout New Mexico, a state with more than 400 years of Spanish heritage and culture. The first Spanish explorers traversed New Mexican lands in 1540, and the earliest colonizers arrived in 1598, establishing the settlement of San Juan de los Caballeros at Ohkay Owingeh Pueblo and what is today Española. In 1609 the settlement was moved to the present-day location of Santa Fe, which became the capital of the interior provinces of the viceroyalty of Nueva España (New Spain). New Mexico remained Spain's northernmost territory for close to 250 years. Spanish language, religion, gastronomy, and artistic and musical heritage were mixed with local Native American traditions, creating a culture that is uniquely New Mexican. Public reenactments, plays, and musical productions, such as *Moros y Cristianos* (Moors and Christians), *Las Posadas* (Joseph and Mary's search for lodging prior to the birth of the Christ child), and the dance of the Matachines, took place in both Native pueblos and Hispano villages throughout the region. Spanish folk songs and dances were passed down from generation to generation, providing a strong foundation for the introduction of flamenco.

In 1821, when Mexico gained independence from Spain, the land that would become New Mexico ceased to be a Spanish colony and became part of the new country of Mexico for twenty-five years. In 1846, the US invasion of Mexican territory instigated the Mexican-American War, which ended with the Treaty of Guadalupe Hidalgo in 1848. All of Mexico's lands north of the Rio Grande, including present-day Arizona, New Mexico, Texas, southern Colorado, and Nevada, were handed over to the United States. New Mexico became a US territory and remained so for another sixty-four years. New Mexico's predominantly Native-speaking people would not become full-fledged US citizens until statehood in 1912.

Peine: Seville, Spain, 2008. Synthetic mother-of-pearl, plastic, metal, glass beads. *Mantón de Manila*: possibly United States, first half of twentieth century. Silk, rayon.

Mantón de Manila: maker unknown, China or Spain, late nineteenth to early twentieth century. Silk, rayon. *Peine*: handmade by Daniel Carnela, La Algaba, Seville, Spain, 2008. Plastic.

Peine by Daniel Carnela.

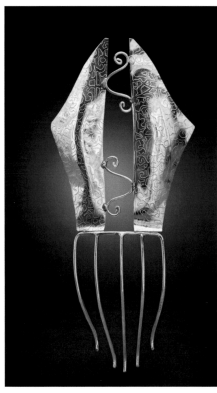

Peine by Antonio Bustamante,
Seville, Spain, 2013.

Spanish Revivals

At the time of New Mexico's statehood, the Spanish craze had already begun on the East Coast and moved westward, bringing an appreciation of Spanish art, music, dance, culture, and architecture. Because of New Mexico's rich Hispano heritage and centuries-old traditions, the Spanish craze did not influence local styles as much as it did in larger cities on the East and West Coasts. However, the craze ultimately grew to incorporate a revival of all things of Spanish heritage throughout the Americas.

One of the manifestations of this revival was Spanish-style architecture, which can be seen in the construction of New York's first Madison Square Garden. Built by architect Stanford White, the structure broke away from neoclassical designs, incorporating instead a rendition of Seville's Islamic-style La Giralda tower. Another version of the tower appeared at the Pan-American Exposition in Buffalo, New York (1901), where it was decorated with thousands of electric lights. By 1928 some twelve versions of La Giralda had been built throughout the United States.[5] The best-known replica still standing is in the Country Club Plaza in Kansas City, which mimics the Plaza de España in Seville. But replicating Spain's prominent buildings was not limited to expositions and public buildings. The 1920s West Coast housing boom produced the California Mission Revival style, which borrowed from Spanish architecture, including elaborate tile work. It was employed by, among others, Bay Area architect Oliver Rousseau, who constructed tract homes with fanciful facades from different countries. Other Spanish re-creations that were popular at the time included architecture patterned after the Alhambra in Granada.

The Spanish craze arrived in New Mexico during the post-railroad period, when products and decorative arts made locally were being threatened by factory-made products, imported fashions, and architectural styles from the East Coast. The result was an effort to preserve local artistic and craft traditions. This wave of historic preservation led to a "new" knowledge of and fascination with all things Spanish. Artists and intellectuals visited or moved to New Mexico in search of an exotic world and a romanticized notion of New Mexican heritage. Locally, New Mexicans began to appreciate their own unique Hispano and Native styles, as well as the value of a growing tourist audience.

Artistic and architectural styles from New Mexico also spread to other parts of the United States. The various replicas of the San Estevan del Rey Mission at Acoma Pueblo provide an example. The first rendition was built in Trinidad, Colorado. Another was constructed as part of the 1915–1916 Panama-California Exposition in San Diego. The New Mexico Museum of Art (formerly the Museum of Fine Arts) in Santa Fe, built in 1917, was based on the San Diego structure.[6] All contributed to a style of architecture now referred to as Pueblo Revival. This revival style combined Native American architectural traditions and Spanish colonial heritage. Prominent in this style of architecture is the stepped design of the walls, the exposed *vigas* (log beams once structural but now purely decorative), multiple rooms with doors facing onto an interior courtyard, and the use of Spanish or Mexican tiles as decorative elements. The courtyards soon became the backdrops for out-of-state and local artists, who portrayed New Mexican señoritas dressed in lace mantillas and embroidered silk shawls.

Santa Fe Fiesta

The popularity of pan-American cultures, as seen in these architectural styles, also manifested in celebrations of Hispano heritage, such as the Fiesta de Los Angeles, which was established in 1895 to honor and celebrate California's Spanish origins.[7] Similar regional celebrations spread across the country, including New Mexico's Fiesta de Santa Fe and other local celebrations. The Santa Fe Fiesta began shortly after statehood and celebrates New Mexico's Hispano history and, more specifically, the reentry of Don Diego de Vargas and his colonizers following the Pueblo Revolt of 1680.[8]

The annual event features the Caballeros de Vargas (Vargas's Gentlemen) and the Reina de la Fiesta (Fiesta Queen) and her court, as well as representatives of the Native American tribes that were allies to the Spanish. The festivities include a procession that reenacts the establishment of Santa Fe as the capital of Nueva Mexico, as well as special church services and processions that honor the Virgin Mary, popularly known as La Conquistadora or "Our Lady Conqueror of Hearts."[9] Along with these historical reenactments, the fiesta's three-day celebration includes the burning of Zozobra (Old Man Gloom), the Desfile de Los Niños (Children's Parade, popularly known as the "Pet Parade"), and the Historical Hysterical Parade. The long weekend continues with music and merriment on the Plaza, a special fashion show, and a *merienda* (light meal or snack) during which traditional Spanish-style hot chocolate and *biscochitos* are served by the Sociedad Colonial (Colonial Society). A special *baile* (dance) and a solemn candlelight procession to the Cross of the Martyrs round out the weekend. Today, the Santa Fe Fiesta is a mix of real and imagined Hispano traditions, which include flamenco and mariachi music, along with Latino rock.[10]

Like the origins of flamenco and the ferias of Andalusia, the seeds of the Santa Fe Fiesta were planted centuries earlier, when the original cohorts of Vargas feared the loss of his legacy within years of his death. In 1712 Captain Juan Paez Hurtado put forth a declaration listing Vargas's accomplishments and calling for an annual fiesta in his honor. The proclamation was signed by New Mexico governor Joseph Chacón Medina Salazar y Villaseñor.[11] Devotion to Vargas and La Conquistadora continued through the centuries, but an official fiesta did not occur until the twentieth century. On September 11, 1919, the first three-day Santa Fe Fiesta opened, and more than ninety-six years later, it is still running strong.

Like the Seville April Fair, no festival is complete without music, costume, and dance. Today, the tradition of attendees dressing up for the Santa Fe Fiesta has died out, but music and merriment have always graced the bandstand and the Plaza.

Dancers on the plaza during the Santa Fe Fiesta, Santa Fe,
New Mexico, 1919.

A typical fiesta performance on the rooftop of La Fonda hotel,
c. 1940s.

A 1947 article in the magazine *New Mexico Music* described the scene: "Music has
played such a major role in the Santa Fe Fiesta, of past and present, that it would
be justifiable to call them musical festivals, as well as historical and religious
events. . . . The combination of music from the old world and the new world, join
to make the Santa Fe Fiesta one of the outstanding yearly musical attractions in the
United States."[12] Throughout the twentieth century, processions and street parades
frequently included marching bands and mariachi music. La Conquistadora was
escorted in a procession accompanied by guitar players and hymns sung in her
honor. Performances of music and dance took place on the rooftop of La Fonda,
a Plaza hotel. Mexican mariachi groups, Spanish folk dancers, big bands, jazz
groups, swing musicians, and popular orchestras were common fixtures. In 1942,
the *New Mexican* described the events on La Fonda's rooftop:

> Following the coronation the spotlights moved to various lower and higher
> roofs where native singers, dancers and musicians proceeded [with] the
> show. Consuelo and Celso Lopez were on the high roof for the tradi-
> tional "Jarabe Tapatio" danced with gay abandon. Nora Chávez, her voice
> never sweeter than over the microphone in the clear air of the night sang
> "Granada," then returned later to provide the vocal accompaniment for the
> pageant of "La Paloma."
> "Paloma" as all in Santa Fe know, is the white dove and it was Mrs.
> Robert L. Wilson and her group of dancers from La Gitana dancing stu-
> dio who provided this beautiful part of the program. Mrs. Wilson and her
> group of dancers were on the high roof, the former dancing with a flutter-
> ing dove, the girls with baskets of flowers on their heads. In the finale the
> girls bent into a circle, then whirled, arms upraised, each with a dove—the
> white birds being released into the black of the night sky.[13]

In the early years, there was elaborate and festive costuming. Performers and
fiesta-goers broke out their best and brightest attire of varying cultural origins.
An annual costume contest ensured that the public would show up in a variety of
finery, and prominent among the costumes were trajes de volantes and *mantóns
de Manila* (shawls from Manila). Much like the mix of Hispano artistic styles that
grew in popularity with the Spanish craze, female fiesta-goers dressed in everything

from the Mexican *china poblana* to lace mantillas draped over Spanish *peinetas* (ornate hair combs). Men dressed as traders along the Santa Fe Trail or in Argentine gaucho attire.[14] Early images show dancers on the Santa Fe Plaza draped in embroidered silk shawls and playing castanets. In September 1919, Jeanette Spiess, a woman of Anglo descent, was named Miss Fair New Mexico. She wore a Spanish silk shawl draped around her body, imitating the flapper attire so prevalent at the time. Native Santa Fean and artist Monica Sosaya Halford fondly remembers when she and her sister Mary dressed up for the weekend activities. Her sister wore the traditional Galician costume native to the region in Spain from which their mother's family came.[15] One of the few events today where participants wear costumes is the Desfile de Los Niños.

The first Fiesta Queen was crowned in 1927, and in the early days they were often Spanish dancers. The 1936 Fiesta Queen was a dancer named Olinda Rodríguez de Castner, who wore a flamenco-style dress made of peach and black taffeta and trimmed in silver sequins. Representing the modern fashion of the time, one side of the dress was slit up to the dropped waist. It came with a matching machine-embroidered silk shawl. In 1947, Spanish dancer Betty Serna Cárdenas was featured on the cover of *New Mexico Music* and a year later was crowned Fiesta Queen. She was one of the last queens to wear the crown of metal and cut-glass stones made by Frank Patania before it was retired to the collections of the Museum of New Mexico. Cárdenas had previously performed in the ceremony of La Paloma

clockwise, top left:
Peine by Justin Gallegos Myrant,
Santa Fe, New Mexico, 2010. Tin.

Peine by Juan López,
Corrales, New Mexico, 2009.
Silver, blue topaz.

Jeanette Spiess, "Miss Fair
New Mexico," 1919. Photograph
by T. Harmon Parkhurst.

Mary Sosaya dressed in a Galician costume for the Fiesta de Santa
Fe, c. 1940. Young New Mexican women often dressed in the regional
attire of their Spanish ancestors. Costume by Angie Sosaya, socks
embroidered by Florence Sosaya (the older sisters of Mary Sosaya).

Fray Angélico Chávez in gaucho costume with Brother Juniper Pappe
during Santa Fe Fiesta, Santa Fe, 1936.

on La Fonda's rooftop with her classmates from La Gitana Studio and also served as a trainbearer for Queen Pita Tapia's court in 1943. One of her favorite memories of her own coronation was the High Mass at the cathedral and the *merienda* that was held in the Museum of Art.[16]

Even though the Fiesta Queen is not always a Spanish dancer, the Hispano musical tradition at the fiesta is alive with performances of Latino rock, mariachi, New Mexican folk music, and flamenco. The inclusion of flamenco has led to its acceptance as a part of New Mexico's traditions and heritage. Even though flamenco was not officially part of the first fiesta in 1919, Spanish dancers draped in their silk shawls and playing castanets graced the Plaza, which led to the incorporation of flamenco into performances throughout the city. The Santa Fe Fiesta's flamenco shows were hosted at St. Francis Auditorium in 1966 and 1967. Lectures and demonstrations took place at the Museum of International Folk Art, including one with singer Miguel Galvez from Spain.[17]

Fiestas throughout the state since the 1960s have also included flamenco.[18] Dancer Lili del Castillo and her husband, guitarist Luís Campos, traveled to the far corners of the state, bringing flamenco to new audiences. They were also on stage for New Mexico's seventy-fifth anniversary celebration of statehood in Albuquerque in 1987.[19] A young dancer from Taos named María Diaz, later known as María Benítez, began her career performing flamenco and Spanish dance at the Taos Fiesta.[20] The closing ceremony of the 400th anniversary of Santa Fe's founding would not have been complete without the inclusion of both flamenco (representing New Mexico's Spanish heritage) and mariachi (representing the state's Mexican heritage). Latino rock rounds out the contemporary trio of Hispano musical traditions, representing the fusion of New Mexico's colonial past and its twenty-first-century cultural diversity.

Chapter 4

Flamenco in New Mexico

I n the early twentieth century, New Mexico was a place where tourists came to visit the exotic "other" without having to leave the country. Fiestas throughout the state celebrated Spanish or Hispano culture and provided performance spaces for dancers and musicians to hone and share their crafts. Folkloric Spanish dance became a staple of New Mexican Hispano culture, along with the romantic image of "Spanish" dancing that looks like or imitates flamenco, which is referred to as "aflamencado."

HISPANO TRADITIONS: AFLAMENCADO TO FLAMENCO

The increasing popularity of Hispano traditions at fiestas and public events throughout New Mexico coincided with the resurgence of traditional, ethnic, and folkloric dancing across the nation. Dance studios and teachers incorporated Spanish and Mexican dancing into their repertoires, along with traditions from Hungary, Greece, and Russia. La Gitana Studio in Santa Fe specialized in classical ballet, jazz, and tap but incorporated Spanish and other ethnic dances into its repertoire. A 1941 recital program from La Gitana illustrates the inclusion of ethnic and folk dancing. Along with ballet numbers and tap dancing, there were dances titled *Hungarian Festival* and *España Cañi*; the latter was a popular paso doble played by brass

Pablo Rodarte and Sara de Luís perform a *garrotín* at the
Flamenco Festival, Albuquerque, New Mexico, 1991.
Photograph by Janet Borelli.

Spanish dancer Betty Serna Cárdenas (left) and unidentified
Mexican dancers greet and perform for the USO in Española, New
Mexico, c. 1947.

opposite:
Dress handmade by Dora Romero, Santa Fe, New Mexico, c. 1947.
The shawl was purchased in Spain in the 1950s.

bands during bullfights in Spain.[1] Dancers and musicians began their educations at
popular cultural events and then continued their studies at community centers and
dance academies like La Gitana. The large number of students, aficionados, and
performers created an accepting environment for the introduction of flamenco in
the mid-twentieth century.

In the early days, academic Spanish dance was a mix of folkloric and classical
dances that employed castanets. Dancers who studied in both Santa Fe and Albuquerque during the 1940s and 1950s remember their dance education as being "a
little bit Mexican, a little bit Spanish." This blending of multiple Hispano cultures
was common throughout the United States at that time.[2] Performances at international fairs and year-end school events often included a variety of pan-American
dances. A 1941 music and dance fiesta at the Santa Fe Indian School showcased
Native American dances along with Mexican and Spanish dances.[3]

Many dancers today recall that in the early years professional education was scarce and that most studios taught a limited amount of Spanish dance and no flamenco. Betty Serna Cárdenas of Santa Fe remembers that when she was a child, Spanish dance education was restricted to small pockets here and there. More often than not, folkloric dancing was a family affair, but dances were sometimes refined in the studio when they were preparing for a performance. In exchange for Cárdenas's lessons at La Gitana Studio, Betty's mother played piano for the classes, and she and Betty's aunt sewed costumes.

Although some instruction in the aflamencado style was available in New Mexico, if students wanted to study seriously they had to leave the state. Since many Spanish immigrants and expatriates settled during and after the Spanish Civil War in New York and Los Angeles, these large cities had a multitude of performance opportunities and were considered the hotbeds for learning Spanish dance.

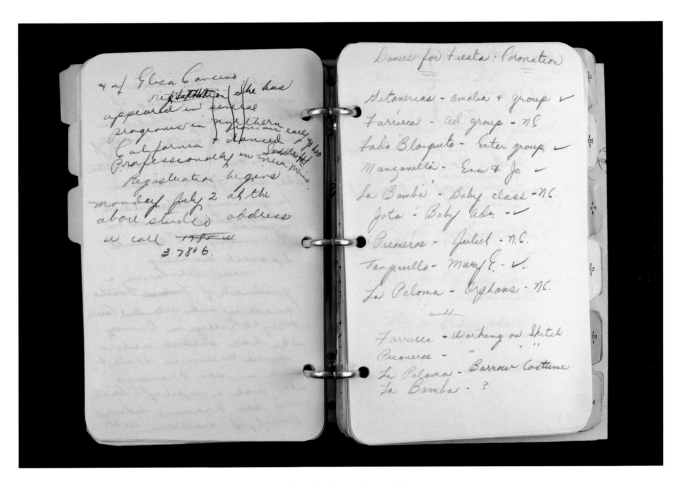

Dance log, c. 1947–1950s, used while Betty Serna Cárdenas was a student under Elisa Cansino in San Francisco and also when she became a teacher in New Mexico. This image shows the variety of regional and classical dances that she performed for the Fiesta de Santa Fe.

After high school graduation, Cárdenas left New Mexico to study ballet at the San Francisco Ballet School. Fortunately, one of the teachers at the academy, Guillermo del Oro, was from Spain and taught classical Spanish dance. While living in San Francisco, Cárdenas also studied privately with Elisa Cansino, a sister of Eduardo and José Cansino of Los Angeles. With both Oro and Cansino, Cárdenas refined her classical training, technique, and castanet skills. She also learned various dance arrangements for popular Spanish music, securing the sheet music from her teachers and taking it home to New Mexico in 1951. She rented a casita in Santa Fe on the property of the Romero family (three siblings of that family eventually became professional flamencos) and opened her own studio, where she taught classes in Spanish dance and ballet.[4] She also was a volunteer instructor at Santa Fe's St. Vincent's Orphanage and traveled regularly to Taos, where she taught at the Taos Inn. She married in 1962 and continued to teach until the birth of her third child.[5]

In Albuquerque Cándido G. García was one of the earliest teachers of Spanish dance. He left New Mexico for the East Coast, where he trained in classical Spanish dance and eventually became a guest artist with the Ziegfeld Follies. During his tenure there, he became good friends with dancer Carmen Amaya. Upon returning to New Mexico, García passed down his formal training to students and future performers. García's nephew Nino García followed in his uncle's footsteps, traveling to New York and playing piano for the José Greco company and the Metropolitan Opera.[6]

Lili del Castillo, who is related to Cándido García on her father's side, began her dance training with Albuquerque's Regina Baca, who taught Spanish dance at the Barelas Community Center. Castillo, who was working at the public library when she noticed an ad for Baca's classes, recalls, "We never did real, traditional flamenco; we did aflamencado-style dancing." She also remembers that most local teachers invented their flamenco steps or movements and that they had little formal training: "There were a lot of creative and innovative ladies making up stuff. They did not know the rigid technique, the complex aspect [of the dance], such as interaction with the guitarist." She describes the transition from the term "Spanish dance" to the word "flamenco": "It was never referred to as 'flamenco' until Sol Hurok brought in the big shows, like those of Carmen Amaya and José Greco."[7]

As noted previously, in the 1940s and 1950s there was an influx of touring Spanish dance companies. Often referred to as *ballets españoles*, these companies showcased a wide variety of Spanish genres, and flamenco was often the grand finale. The companies of Amaya and Greco were the first to present shows that were entirely flamenco, introducing the idea of "Gypsy flamenco" to the nation. The art form, which had originated in the informal setting of the home, moved elegantly into the realm of theatrical art. Outside of New Mexico, the dance became codified, and official steps and movements were taught in Spain and larger US metropolitan areas. Dancers and musicians like Cándido and Nino García, who trained formally and worked in large dance companies, began differentiating between flamenco and the other Spanish dances.

Lili del Castillo at age fifteen performing at the Gazebo in Old
Town, Albuquerque, New Mexico, c. 1958.

Regina Baca directed a pre-professional company called the Tiny Señoritas,
which consisted of school-age girls, including Castillo, who was in high school and
the oldest performer at the time. Baca's company was Castillo's first foray into the
world of performing. Vivian Alarid Cuadra joined Baca's group at the age of eight.
As a child, she was taken to see several of Hurok's touring shows, including those
featuring Carmen Amaya and José Greco, although she was so young she does not
remember Amaya.[8] The Tiny Señoritas were invited to Los Angeles in 1959 for the
Convention of the National Federation of Musicians, and they also had the honor

of being the first Spanish dance group to perform at Disneyland, just after its first major renovation and grand reopening—a memory that lasted a lifetime for the young dancers from Albuquerque.[9]

Upon returning home, members of the Tiny Señoritas were excited about continuing their training, but there were not many professionals teaching flamenco at the time. Baca learned that Cándido García had stopped touring and had returned to New Mexico. She invited him to teach her students how to play the castanets, and they soon were learning the various genres of folkloric and classical Spanish dance. Until then the girls had caught their only glimpse of traditional flamenco when Hurok brought companies to New Mexico. Castillo recalls seeing the Ximenez-Vargas company and their rendition of the *petenera* (a song from the cante jondo genre), which is to this day one of her favorites. In 1962, Hurok brought José Greco's company to Albuquerque, and the show included an appearance by fourteen-year-old Paco de Lucía, who later became one of the top guitarists in the world. Members of the Tiny Señoritas attended a special reception, and the girls were honored to greet Greco and his company.[10]

The Tiny Señoritas welcome José Greco to Albuquerque, New Mexico, 1968.

Album cover, *The Golden Strings of Ramón Hernández*, c. 1960s.

The Music of - Bach • Tarrega • Sor • Almeida and others

The Golden Strings of **Ramon** *Hernandez*

In the early 1960s, performances of flamenco and classical Spanish music by local artists were uncommon. One of the earliest regular performers was Taos guitarist Ramón Hernández, the namesake of Ramón's Tavern, where he played nightly. He had studied guitar in Los Angeles with Vicente Gómez, who had played in the movie *Blood and Sand* (discussed above).[11] Hernández was possibly the first New Mexican to record a Spanish guitar album.

Guitarist Luís Campos recalls seeing Hernández perform at the Carriage Inn in Los Alamos. The music reminded him of the famous guitarist Sabicas, whose music he had heard on the radio as a child—sounds so haunting and mesmerizing that he never forgot them. As a child, Campos moved with his family from Los Alamos to the San Diego area, where he had the good fortune of studying with members of the flamenco company of Leonor Amaya (sister of Carmen), who moved between Los Angeles and Tijuana, Mexico. Campos eventually played guitar for flamenco classes taught by Amaya's dance partner Juan Martín and her singer El Niño Brillante (Bright Child).[12] Upon his return to Los Alamos in 1961, Campos looked for opportunities to continue studying and performing classical Spanish and flamenco guitar. He soon met a dancer recently returned from Spain who was starting his own troupe: Vicente Romero, who came to be known as the godfather of flamenco dance in Northern New Mexico.

VICENTE ROMERO: DAZZLING DANCE AND INSPIRATION

Vicente Romero was born in Santa Fe on April 13, 1937, the oldest of five siblings. Growing up in a musical family, he was a student of modern dance and had just begun his studies of Spanish dance when he saw the film *Sombrero* featuring José Greco. Then and there, Romero decided he wanted to be a Spanish dancer, and at age fifteen, after much debate with his parents, he left for Los Angeles to study with the Cansinos. Soon, dancer Lola Montes saw Romero perform and invited him to join her company. He toured with Montes for several years, and at one point had an encounter with Greco. Not a man to miss talent when he saw it, Greco encouraged Romero to continue his career and told him, "If you're serious, young man, go to Spain."[13]

Pubicity shot of Vicente Romero in his classic masculine stance, c. 1957. Photograph by Miguel Angel Yanez.

Romero left for Spain in 1957 with the financial support of British actress and philanthropist Greer Garson, who had retired to New Mexico. Romero's first performance in Madrid was an improvisational act, and Pilar López happened to be in the audience. López invited the twenty-year-old Romero to join her company—he was only the second American to do so—following in the footsteps of José Greco.[14] For the next five years Romero toured throughout Europe and Asia with the Ballet Español Pilar López. He left the company in 1961 and took on a six-month contract as a dancer and choreographer for a flamenco group that included Nana Lorca, who previously had danced as Greco's leading lady, and Roberto Lorca, who had toured with Lola Montes's company. With them, Romero performed throughout the United States, Canada, and Puerto Rico.[15] He later joined the company of José Greco. Upon returning to the United States, Romero performed in front of an audience of 19,000 at Madison Square Garden. Much in demand, his whirlwind schedule eventually caught up with him. Shortly after the Madison Square Garden concert, health issues forced him to cancel a four-week engagement at New York's Chateau Madrid and return to New Mexico for rest and recuperation.[16]

Recovered and planning for the future, Romero developed a new performance venue and several educational programs in New Mexico. One of his earliest shows, which took place at the Los Alamos Civic Auditorium on August 26, 1963, was titled *Guitar, Lorca, and Flamenco*. Romero brought in guitarist Hector García as a special guest and also included local performers Lili del Castillo and Luís Campos. (Lili and Luís married a year later and, with the encouragement of Romero, went to Spain for further study.)[17] A letter to the editor written by Bea Thompson of Los Alamos raved about the performance, although she lamented the fact that the auditorium was not filled to brimming: "Los Alamos people didn't know what they missed last evening with the performance of the Romero Troupe at Civic Auditorium. The magnificent performance held the half filled theatre spellbound. . . . During the guitar presentations you could hear a pin drop. Romero knew the audience enjoyed his staccato footwork and broke his scheduled numbers to give another display of this precision work. A REAL AUDIENCE PLEASER."[18] The fact that the theater was not full illustrates that small-town audiences still needed to be educated about concert-style flamenco performances.

Romero continued producing theatrical shows, developing in the process a large following of local, national, and international audiences. Two years after his first show in Los Alamos, he returned there and also presented his show at St. John's College in Santa Fe on August 4, 1965. One critic wrote, "I know of no other male Spanish dancer alive today who can compare to Vicente Romero. His natural grace, the infinite variety of his *taconeo* [heel tapping], his extraordinary understatement when he dances—all these qualities and many others remind me of the greatest of the Spanish dancers of old."[19]

After performing in a concert with guitarists Luís Campos and Hector García at Santa Fe's St. Francis Auditorium, Romero was approached by Ray Arias, who

Program for El Nido's flamenco show, Tesuque, New Mexico, c. 1965.

owned El Nido (Bird's Nest), a popular restaurant and watering hole in nearby Tesuque. In the summer of 1964 at El Nido, the first tablao-style show in New Mexico featured Romero, who did two sets of flamenco performances, one at 9:00 p.m. and the second at 11:00 p.m. These first performances were in the Zozobra room, where the backdrop was a large painting of Zozobra by local artist Will Shuster. That first year, Romero brought in singer and dancer Roberto Canas as the featured artist. The other company members were local dancers Victoria Quijada, Carla Duran, and Isabela Otero, and guitarists Juan Nadas, Roberto Millet, Eric Patterson, and Vicente's brother Ruben Romero.[20]

The flamenco shows at El Nido grew in popularity, and to accommodate the growing crowds, they were moved to an interior courtyard that had a tree in the middle, which was named El Patio Flamenco. For his third summer season in 1966, Romero invited Lydia Torea, a colleague from Spain and his touring days, as a guest artist. Their show opened to acclaim, with photos featured in the *New Mexican* on more than one occasion and one headline referring to "two of the world's fastest rising stars."[21] Another article claimed, "The show, which opened June 13, has drawn press notices throughout the state, in addition to Arizona, Colorado and talent scouts from at least three show places in Las Vegas, Nev."[22] Torea was already renowned for dancing alongside José Greco in the film *Ship of Fools*, and Romero too was a star. Prior to the 1966 summer season, he had been introduced to Art Linkletter by Greer Garson. Linkletter, who was impressed with Romero's performances at El Nido, invited him to perform as one of the stars on the nationally televised show *Hollywood Talent Scout*.[23] Garson served as Romero's sponsor and introduced him to the audience.

The dynamic duo of Vicente Romero and Lydia Torea during a performance at El Nido, Tesuque, New Mexico, 1966.

The shows at El Nido were a burst of flamenco light that dazzled for more than a decade. A 1966 description in the *New Mexican* stated, "More than 125 persons crowded into the Flamenco Patio at El Nido in Tesuque for the opening of the summer-long season of the Festival Flamenco last night, and in spite of the over-crowded conditions, witnessed what has to be one of the finest exhibitions of true traditional Flamenco ever to hit the city of Santa Fe or perhaps the entire South-west."[24] Of Torea and Romero's partnership, the writer exclaimed, "never before it seems have two great dancers, Ms. Torea and Romero, with natural talent—and hard work—ever showed to an audience such a complete control and communica-tion between each other as exhibited in their dances. Individually each is an expert, but combined they are fantastic." Torea was described as "a dancer par excellence" who possessed the ability "to create or change a mood with her eyes. . . . The ex-pressions she applies to her dancing talents are a thing of sheer beauty." Romero "performed routines that were extremely taxing on one's stamina but not once did he show signs of running out of steam."[25] Another writer also complimented Romero's talent: "Today Romero is being touted by critics, not only in the United States but in Spain where he does a lot of study and work, as the 'heir apparent' to the throne as 'King of Flamenco.'"[26]

Following the 1966 summer season at El Nido, Romero continued the tradition of showcasing flamenco and Spanish dance during the Santa Fe Fiesta. The first of two fiesta-themed shows opened at St. Francis Auditorium with Torea as the guest artist. The group gave three performances during the fiesta weekend of September 2–3.[27] Torea was also the guest artist with Romero for a show sponsored by the Los Alamos Opera Guild. The production, titled *Festival Flamenco*, was a benefit for the Santa Fe Opera.[28] The duo also presented their show at the University of New Mexico with a company of eight dancers and singers in 1966.[29] The group then took off for performances at the Third Eye Theater in Denver and at the Sands Hotel in Las Vegas. The 1966 season proved to be a great success for Romero and Torea, and their artistic collaboration lasted for several years.

The 1967 season was also prosperous for Romero's El Nido and Santa Fe Fiesta concerts. He brought in guitarist René Heredia, who was of Gitano and Spanish decent. Heredia grew up in the United States and gained experience playing for Carmen Amaya.[30] Romero's company also included his brother Miguel, dancer Carla Duran, and the duo Choly and Isabel from Spain. The concert again took place at St. Francis Auditorium.[31]

The shows at El Nido not only served as entertainment for tourists and locals, but they also provided an atmosphere where performers and aficionados interacted, exchanged ideas, and learned from each other. Romero scouted out talent in Spain

Vicente Romero and troupe were featured in the July 1970 issue of *New Mexico Magazine*. *Left to right*: Vicente Romero, María Benítez, Carla Duran, Miguel Romero.

and the United States and brought top-quality performers to New Mexico. A few of his musicians were American artists who had lived and studied in Spain at the same time as Romero. Guest artists from Spain who were staying in Santa Fe for the summer season provided lessons in guitar playing, singing, and dancing. One of the most favored forms of flamenco education was the all-night juerga (flamenco jam session). Guitarist David Briggs, originally from Boston, moved to New Mexico after traveling and studying in Spain. He had heard about the state's "flamenco atmosphere" from his guitar teacher. He still recalls the exchange of ideas, the live improvised music, and the party atmosphere: "It was like being back in Spain. Those were the days!"[32]

Romero's brothers Ruben and Miguel received their earliest flamenco education performing in his El Nido shows and jamming alongside top guitarists from Spain. Both became acclaimed flamenco and Spanish classical guitarists. The boys grew up on the same property where Betty Serna Cárdenas rented a casita for her first dance studio. Their father was a violinist who played with many local artists during the Santa Fe Fiesta. Growing up in Santa Fe, the boys were accustomed to hearing Spanish music at local celebrations but were unfamiliar with traditional flamenco. Ruben heard his first sevillanas at age seven at the Taos Inn, but both boys were more interested in playing rock an' roll using a steel-string guitar that they shared.[33] When Vicente returned to New Mexico in 1961, he encouraged them to learn flamenco and soon asked Ruben, just sixteen at the time, to be one of his accompanists at El Nido. Playing alongside some of the top guitarists from Spain, Ruben was particularly inspired by Manolo Vásquez and took lessons from Luís Campos during the off-season. Miguel and Ruben both toured in the Southwest and played with the Minnesota Orchestra and the Denver Symphony with Miguel Galvez, whom they met while working with Vicente.

El Nido's visiting guitarists were also a boon to others who came to New Mexico to partake of the flamenco scene. Guitarists Bruce and Eric Patterson, originally from Los Angeles, played at El Nido alongside Ruben and Miguel Romero and Luís Campos. Bruce had met Vicente while both were living and working in Spain. Taking the name El Niño Dorado (Golden Boy), he played several seasons at El Nido and also for special concert-style performances. Although Bruce did not remain in New Mexico, Eric pursued a career of playing for performances and teaching classes at the University of New Mexico.

During the 1960s, flamenco *cante* (singing) was foreign to US audiences. The performer's raspy vocalizations and intense outbursts sounded like yelling to the untrained ear. Romero knew that singers were a critical component of a high-energy flamenco performance, and he made sure to include top singers from Andalusia in his shows. In addition to performing at El Nido, several did concert-style performances that further demonstrated their talents. In a tablao-style flamenco show, the cantaor and the dancer have a back-and-forth exchange, necessitating rules of technique and structure in the music so that the dancer, the singer, and the guitarist all communicate. In a concert setting, the singer is able to flow freely, showing off his or her wares without worrying about the structure of the dance. Singer Miguel Galvez from Seville appeared in the 1966 summer season, which he ended with a special performance at the Museum of International Folk Art, accompanied by El Niño Dorado on guitar. It was one of Santa Fe's first lecture-demonstrations on flamenco's history. Romero introduced the program, and Galvez presented the different styles of flamenco song, including *cante grande*, those of more somber moods, and *cante chico*, lighter songs in a more festive style.[34]

ENCOUNTERS: CONNECTIONS AND COLLABORATIONS

After El Nido's shows concluded for the summer, Romero produced touring shows and conducted programs during the off-season around the state. One year he joined Suzanne M. Johnston's New Mexico Ballet Company in Albuquerque and applied for a grant from the New Mexico Arts Commission, seeking funds for a collaboration in which the pair would fuse various dance styles. Under a federal program, Romero also offered lecture-demonstrations throughout Northern New Mexico. Explaining his interest in educational programs, Romero said that he liked speaking to kids in Spanish, the language often spoken in their homes, and as a native New Mexican, he felt a kinship with the local populations.[35]

Local musicians also benefited from Romero's visiting artists and developing flamenco scene. David Briggs recalls the similarities between José Greco and Vicente Romero. Both were dashing on stage and off, and they shared an affinity for bringing together artists who under other circumstances might not work together and putting them on stage to create one fantastic performance after another. Both also inspired younger artists by including them in the chorus or as extras in their companies. The young artists learned from the top performers and, in many instances, went on to careers in the flamenco performance world. The paths of many of these performers often crossed later, resulting in inspired collaborations over the years.[36]

Romero always encouraged students and members of his company to travel to Spain and experience firsthand the culture in which flamenco was born, especially if they aspired to a professional flamenco career. In an era before email and the internet, Romero knew how to network, and he wrote formal letters of introduction, which often opened doors to further study and a professional career. While in Madrid, Romero introduced Lydia Torea to Maruja Martín Mayor, a patron of the arts with a particular interest in propagating flamenco. He also provided a letter of introduction to Mayor for guitarist Luís Campos and dancer Lili del Castillo when they studied in Spain. When Torea took over the 1972 summer season at El Nido, Castillo was invited to be one of the dancers.

Dancer Teo Morca, who met Romero while on tour with the company of Lola Montes, was also encouraged by Romero to study in Spain. Like Greco and

above:
Luís Campos (*left*) in an impromptu *juerga* with Luís Huertas on the ship *Guadalupe* en route to Spain, 1964. Lili del Castillo is seated in the background, resting between dances.

Lili del Castillo (foreground) performing with Lydia Torea and Bob Rich at El Nido, Tesuque, New Mexico, 1971.

opposite:
Bata de cola (flamenco dress with train), Madrid, Spain, c. 1965. Polyester, nylon, cotton.

Romero, Morca was performing in one of his first televised jobs in Spain when he was discovered by Pilar López, who asked him to join her company. Morca also worked as a choreographer in New York and Los Angeles and worked with a trio that included New Mexico dancer María Diaz (later Benítez). Morca collaborated with Benítez briefly in Madrid, and when she decided to continue her studies in Spain, Morca took over her summer performance season in Taos. Subsequently, they went their separate ways: Morca married dancer Isabel Grijalva, who performed as Isabel Morca, and opened a studio in Bellingham, Washington, where he conducted some of the earliest all-flamenco workshops in the country. Benítez went on to become one of the biggest flamenco stars New Mexico has ever seen.[37]

MARÍA BENÍTEZ: ELECTRIC PERFORMER, DYNAMIC MENTOR

María Benítez was originally named María Woesha (Girl Bringer of Happiness). Her mother, Geraldine D. Harvey, was of Chippewa and Oneida heritage, and her father, Josue Eliu Diaz, was of Puerto Rican descent. Benítez grew up in Taos Pueblo, where her mother was a teacher and the first Native American to receive a master's degree. Early on Benítez studied piano and classical ballet with Louise Licklider.[38] She knew of Spanish and aflamencado dancing, but her dream was to become a ballet dancer. After Benítez's ballet classmate Cecilia Torres shared what she had learned from studying in Los Angeles with the Cansinos, Benítez realized that she "did not have the figure, nor the temperament" for ballet and decided to pursue Spanish dance.[39]

She began performing with Ramón Hernández at his tavern and in shows at Taos's Sagebrush Inn. She also danced on the plaza during the Fiesta de Taos. Her early choreographies were the *farruca*, a serious dance that was once only performed by men, and a classical piece to *Malagueña* by Cuban composer Ernesto Lecuona. Continuing her studies, Benítez trained with Denver teacher Louise Campos while attending a small private school in Colorado. This training proved confusing for Benítez, however, because Campos's style was completely different from that of the Cansinos, which Benítez had learned from Torres. Campos taught a folkloric style of dancing, while the Cansinos style was more footwork-heavy and flamenco-based. Benítez realized that she would have to go to the cradle of flamenco to learn the intricacies of the dance.[40]

In 1963, at age nineteen, with the support of her mother, Benítez went to Spain and stayed for five years. She began her studies with Victoria Eugenia, who had danced in the company of Antonio "El Chavalillo" (formerly of the duo Rosario and Antonio). Eugenia oversaw a formal academy, and her style of dancing included specific arm structure and posturing. Benítez learned Eugenia's style and adopted it throughout her career. After six months of study, Benítez obtained her first job in the company of María Rosa, with whom she spent the next several years training and dancing, followed by joining the company of Paquita Rico. She also met and performed with other American dancers, initiating what would become future partnerships and guest appearances.

While in Madrid, María married Cecilio Benítez. Originally from the town of Arenys de Mar in the province of Barcelona, Cecilio was working in Madrid as a theater technician when the two met. They returned to New Mexico in 1967 for the birth of their son Francisco. They produced a show for the Taos Art Association and regularly performed at La Fonda in Taos. Realizing they needed a more stable income to raise their young child, the couple moved to Sedona, Arizona, and both took teaching positions.[41] At Sedona's Valley Verde School, Cecilio taught Spanish literature and directed plays, and María taught ballet and modern dance. María also served as a guest teacher at the Boston Conservatory of Music and the University of Utah. When asked to perform in a solo concert showcasing flamenco for Valley Verde School, she realized that she missed the stage and the hours spent in the studio perfecting her technique.[42] Unable to find a guitarist near Sedona, the couple

María Benítez and Vicente Romero performing at El Nido, Tesuque, New Mexico, c. 1970.

María Benítez and Vicente Romero demonstrating the sensuality of partner dancing in flamenco, Tesuque, New Mexico, c. 1970.

returned to New Mexico and soon María met Vicente Romero and began dancing as his partner in the flamenco shows at El Nido. The combination of the two dancers from New Mexico—Romero from Santa Fe and Benítez from Taos—was an instant success. Audiences raved, and they appeared together on the cover of *New Mexico Magazine*.[43] To this day, many flamencos who were present at the time remember their dynamism on stage and consider their partnership to have been one of the best. Briggs recalls with a sparkle in his eye that "she was the best partner he ever had; they went together perfectly."[44]

In 1971, after seven successful years, Romero broke away from El Nido to start a new tablao-style show called La Zambra at El Gancho (the present-day Steaksmith at El Gancho) off Old Las Vegas Highway in Santa Fe. Jorge Midon, a former professional dancer from Argentina, became Romero's business partner and also manager of the establishment. In an early press release, Midon discussed the partnership and new venture: "We hope to make a contribution to establish Santa Fe as a center for flamenco in the U.S."[45] Once the shows at La Zambra were established, Romero handed over the 1971 summer season at El Nido to Torea, who shared billing with partner Felipe de la Rosa. They had arrived in New Mexico fresh from two world tours with the famous guitarist and comedienne Charo and the Latin American superstar Xavier Cugat.

In 1972, after Romero had moved to La Zambra, Benítez established her own company called Estampa Flamenca: María Benítez Teatro Flamenco. She and Cecilio moved permanently back to New Mexico and soon took over at El Nido. Her performances were frequently sold out, and she kept the establishment at the top of tourist itineraries. By the 1972 season, El Nido was billing itself as "the original home of flamenco in the Southwest," perhaps in competition with the new venue, La Zambra, which had opened on the opposite side of Santa Fe.[46] Even though Romero and Benítez had their own nightly shows, they still collaborated for special performances. They starred together in *Tablao Flamenco* in 1974 at Popejoy Hall in Albuquerque, where they were joined by Chenin de Triana from Spain, René Heredia, and Miguel and Ruben Romero.[47]

Like Romero, Benítez was a local celebrity. By the time of her Santa Fe Opera debut in 1975 in Verdi's *La Traviata*, she had become a household name. On opening night, she and her dance company stole the show, receiving accolades from music critics in Denver, San Diego, and San Francisco. Benítez considered her opera performances some of the most important of her career, and they secured her footing as the star of flamenco in Santa Fe. She was invited to perform at the New York Dance Festival at the Delacorte Theater in September 1975. Her success attested to the

María Benítez and her newly formed company, Estampa Flamenca: María Benítez Teatro Flamenco, at El Nido, Tesuque, New Mexico, 1972.

recognition of her talent and the fascination on the East Coast with a real flamenco dancer from the Southwest. The romantic image of Hispano culture was still alive.

New York was a turning point in Benítez's career and put her "on the map."[48] She had spent years touring Spain and Latin America, but she did not move out of the "local Santa Fe dancer" category until her New York debut. At that time she and Cecilio decided to get an apartment in New York and hire a management company, although they retained their home in Santa Fe. As she put it, "Without management, you are dead in the water."[49] The couple teamed up with producer-agent Harry Rubenstein, and Benítez received invitations to perform with her company at summer dance festivals all along the East Coast. They also performed at New York's Joyce Theater and the Kennedy Center in Washington, DC; and they traveled to Canada, Germany, and the Netherlands. Her first year in New York also saw the nationwide release of the PBS special *Estampa Flamenca*.

Benítez stayed at El Nido for a total of four years and then moved to La Zambra once Romero left the establishment to teach privately. The summer seasons in Santa Fe lasted for close to three months and roughly coincided with the opera season. Her final performances each summer were held on the same weekend as the Santa Fe Fiesta. The rest of the year, María Benítez Teatro Flamenco toured the nation and the globe.

These costumes were owned and danced by María Benítez. Vest by Vargas, Madrid, Spain, c. 1965. Silk, cotton, beads, metallic thread, sequins.

Vest by Fermín, Madrid, Spain, c. 1980. Cotton velveteen, rayon, metallic sequins, beads.

Falda (skirt) by Pies de Resistance, Madrid, Spain, c. 1964.
Polyester, cotton, nylon.

opposite:
Traje flamenca (flamenco costume) by Costa Cortijo, Madrid,
Spain, c. 1965. Polyester, nylon.

This *Bata de cola* (shown with a *mantón de Manila*) was featured on the cover of *Dance Magazine*. Handmade by Luís Rodríguez (aka Paca la Brava), New York, 1970s.

With its Spanish roots, New Mexico was the perfect place for flamenco, and Benítez considered it the US equivalent of southern Spain—"a place where the world visits to study, enjoy, and stretch the bounds of flamenco."[50] For Benítez, staying in Santa Fe provided stability and a sense of home. Company members from Spain also enjoyed staying in one location for an entire season. Benítez described her residency in New Mexico as a time of reflection. In an interview in *Dance Magazine* she said, "You have to know where you stand within the universe. I go out to New Mexico, and I see that country—those mountains, those sunsets—and it's a whole different feel, a place to gain, or regain, perspective." She also showed an appreciation for performing in front of New Mexican audiences: "After fourteen years, I have built an audience; they come to see the show—and you can hear a pin drop! It wasn't always like that. I remember doing a lot of shows for which there were four or five people in the audience. . . . But I proved myself, and they're very loyal to me in Santa Fe. The audience is always with me, and it can be a hard audience to win over."[51] In another interview she said, "I'm most nervous when I dance there [Santa Fe]. It's the home-turf audience."[52]

FLAMENCO MECCA

Dancers like Romero and Benítez, along with the many other artists who settled in New Mexico during the 1960s, made New Mexico a popular destination for tourists and aficionados. Establishments that showcased flamenco also included the cuisine of Spain and were filled with the ambience of Andalusia. Flamencos frequented these venues and watched each other's shows, and Spanish was heard everywhere. Students also became regulars, seeking the feel and the knowledge of the flamenco community in Spain. With establishments such as El Nido and La Zambra on secure footing, the flamenco community in New Mexico grew during the 1970s, and there was a widespread spirit of collaboration. Along with nightly gigs, larger productions took place in the northern parts of the state and in Albuquerque. In 1973 Lili del Castillo presented New Mexico's first flamenco dance drama, *Feria*, which told the history of New Mexico via flamenco and Native American dance. The show opened to mixed reviews; one critic referred to it as an "outrageous presentation of *intercultural* music and dance based on New Mexico legends."[53] Castillo remembers it as a major personal accomplishment that required more work than her regular restaurant gigs, but she also laughingly recalls that "Vicente [Romero] walked out of the show."[54]

From 1972 to 1974, Luís Campos played live concerts regularly in the Kachina Room at the Albuquerque airport. In 1975 Romero brought Torea back for a special concert-style performance that included his brothers Ruben and Miguel. This *Festival Flamenco* was staged at University of New Mexico's Keller Hall. The show had a cast of eight dancers, singers, and musicians, including Teo Morca and Luís Campos.[55] La Fonda hotel in Santa Fe began nightly performances in La Plazuela dining room with Campos on guitar, while on the weekend full tablao-style shows were performed by Campos and Castillo and their newly formed group, Rincón Flamenco. The duo also joined dancer Elizabeth Luján, a former member of the Tiny Señoritas, and her Gypsy cantaor husband, José Arencón, known as "Pelete," for weekend performances at the historic High Noon Restaurant and Saloon in Old Town, Albuquerque, where live flamenco guitar shows continue to this day.

When La Fonda began hosting flamenco groups, Benítez left La Zambra and moved her show there. In Albuquerque, concerts were held in conjunction with Hispano programs at the University of New Mexico, and the Los Alamos Opera Guild continued its annual fundraiser, *A Night of Guitar, Lorca, and Flamenco*, in which many of New Mexico's artists, both local and transplants, such as Bruce Patterson and Carlos Lomas, continued to perform. (For one such concert in 1980, Benítez's company brought in the world-famous master of guitar Emilio Prados.)[56] Briggs remembers those times fondly. He and his wife built a dance studio behind their home, which was frequented by dancers and musicians on a nightly basis.[57] He recalls that the flamenco spirit was so strong that people who normally did not get along in other settings jammed together, sharing new musical riffs and techniques.[58]

In 1980 guitarist Carlos Lomas arrived in Santa Fe for Benítez's summer season at La Fonda. Lomas had spent ten years in Spain, playing at some of the top flamenco tablaos and touring. After returning to the United States, he joined José Greco's company as one of the lead guitarists, and in New Mexico he felt right at home. At this time he also met his future wife and collaborator the singer-dancer Gioia Tama, who regularly performed with Vicente Romero. Of the scene at the time, he recalls, "I fell in love with New Mexico. It reminded me of Spain; many people still spoke Spanish here!"[59] In the summer of 1981, Benítez moved back to La Zambra, and Lomas brought in Greco to perform at La Fonda. Lomas remembers that both shows went on six nights a week: "There were enough people in Santa Fe to support both groups simultaneously."[60] Each company had a different night off, and the performers often went to see each other's shows.

By the middle of the 1980s both El Nido and La Zambra had ceased to exist, but live flamenco performances continued at Santa Fe's La Fonda. In 1985, María and Cecilio Benítez moved their show to the Sheraton Hotel (now the Lodge at Santa Fe). There they established a small nightclub setting and continued to bring in top artists from Spain. At the same time, their Institute for Spanish Arts, an organization established in 1974 and dedicated to the preservation of Spanish dance and music, gained additional financial support and momentum. Under the umbrella

An early publicity shot of guitarist David Briggs (aka El Niño David), Boston, Massachusetts, c. 1963. Photograph by Eddie Freeman.

Gioia Tema and Vicente Romero perform at El Santuario de Guadalupe, Santa Fe, New Mexico, 1981. Photograph by Jane Grossenbacher.

of the organization, guest artists who performed in the nightly shows also conducted two-week master workshops, allowing local up-and-coming dancers to learn
flamenco firsthand. María and Cecilio traveled regularly to Spain, visiting relatives
and scouting the best and brightest talent to bring to New Mexico.[61]

When not in Santa Fe, company members toured the country, appearing at
dance festivals and theaters. Benítez's shows sold out on a regular basis, and she
continued to receive rave reviews. Echoing the responses to early performances by
José Greco, who also was not a native Spaniard, her 1986 performance at the Joyce
Theater was described this way: "Artistically she is so authentic, so hot and steamy,
so vibrant, one could easily assume she was raised in the heart of Spain."[62] For her
1988 season at the Joyce, Benítez brought in Greco as a guest artist—the first time
the two greats had performed together. The performance was remembered two
years later: "In the 1988 appearance of María Benítez's Spanish Dance Company,
she was joined by José Greco as a guest star. Benítez's courtesy during that performance was a joy to experience. In a sense, they honored each other." The critic
went on: "Having been born in Italy and raised in Brooklyn he [Greco] proved that
you need not be a gypsy, nor even Spanish, to pursue flamenco dancing as a theatrical art. María Benítez, of American Indian and Puerto Rican parentage, is further
proof of Greco's trailblazing demonstration."[63] The same reviewer had described
Benítez's 1989 season at the Joyce: "Now in her 40s, Benítez was in top expressive
form; she managed to be earthy and elegant, deep and flashy, sensual and strong,
intense and beguiling, concentrated and playing to the audience, at once. The inner
and outer are balanced in her."[64] National and international fame followed: Benítez
received the Governor's Award for Excellence in the Arts, appeared in *Vogue*
magazine, performed with the Boston Pops, and was a guest artist on one of Perry
Como's Christmas specials on television.

FESTIVAL FLAMENCO INTERNACIONAL DE ALBUQUERQUE
Many of the artists who came to New Mexico either remained in the state
or returned on several occasions. Studios throughout the state offered classes in
Spanish, in aflamencado-style dancing, and in traditional flamenco, including the
two-week dance workshops put on by the Institute for Spanish Arts. However, most
students and aficionados were still hungry for more. In Albuquerque, a burgeoning
flamenco scene took off when a young dancer of Spanish and New Mexican heritage named Eva Enciñias-Sandoval came to the University of New Mexico.

Enciñias-Sandoval grew up in Albuquerque hearing Spanish songs in the
house. Her mother, Clarita García de Aranda (a relative of Cándido and Nino
García), was a singer and dance instructor who began passing the tradition to her
daughter. Clarita had learned Spanish songs and folk dances from her mother,
Juana Candelaria, who had learned from relatives in Spain.[65] While still a young
child, Eva learned the same classical, folkloric, and traditional songs, but she soon

began to concentrate on flamenco. She performed with her mother and studied with flamencos such as Teo Morca. As a student at the University of New Mexico, she suggested that the Theatre and Dance Department include flamenco as a genre, and by 1976 the university was the first in the country to offer flamenco classes, which were taught by Enciñias-Sandoval. At the university she created Alma Flamenca, a pre-professional group of dancers picked from her advanced classes. She and her mother also began their first professional dance troupe, Ritmo Flamenco (Flamenco Rhythm).

By the mid-1980s, Ritmo Flamenco (which included two male UNM dance students, Paco Antonio and Cristobal de la O), was performing regularly around the state. An announcement for a show in April 1986 noted: "Ritmo has incorporated imaginative accompaniments ranging from hammers on an anvil to classical Vivaldi in its exploration of Flamenco. The spectrum of possibilities requires the diverse foundations in ballet and modern dance possessed by members of the dance

An early playbill for Eva Enciñias-Sandoval's group Ritmo Flamenco, 1986.

troupe. . . . The elegant suites performed by Ritmo include breathtaking solos, intimate duets, and grand ensemble works. Ritmo transcends traditional expectations while respecting the haunting beauty that is Flamenco."[66] The same article described Enciñias-Sandoval: "With this extensive background, she has blended the essence of various styles into a personal approach to Flamenco that is . . . bold in its expression. . . . She has received high acclaim for her innovative choreography and her remarkable performance ability."[67]

Other flamenco artists and musicians also established their own groups, such as Los Serranos of Santa Fe, which was formed in 1979 and included native New Mexican Susannah Garrett, guitarist David Briggs, guitarist Peter Culbert (aka Pedro el Abogado, Peter the Attorney), and dancer-singer Tamara S'pagnola. Groups met and exchanged ideas for dance steps and choreographies, and new guitar riffs were tried out among like-minded friends and aficionados. At one such gathering in the home of Lili del Castillo and Luís Campos, the seeds for a New Mexican flamenco festival were planted. Enciñias-Sandoval, who had attended the flamenco workshops put on by Morca in Bellingham, Washington, and brought him to New Mexico in 1983 to serve as a guest teacher for UNM master classes, presented the idea to Castillo.[68] Enciñias-Sandoval proposed a two-week all-flamenco gathering, which would include performances showcasing New Mexican dancers and musicians and a special guest or two from outside the state. Castillo, who was actively performing in Santa Fe and in contact with the flamenco community in Northern New Mexico, invited Santa Fe performers to a meeting set up by Enciñias-Sandoval.[69] Enciñias-Sandoval then asked the University of New Mexico to host the first Festival Flamenco Internacional de Albuquerque (International Flamenco Festival of Albuquerque). The university saw the festival as a public relations opportunity, not only for the university and its dance programs, but for the state and Albuquerque in particular. The first Albuquerque Festival took place on July 17–18, 1987. Eleven years later, the UNM Theatre and Dance Department established a BA program in dance with an emphasis in flamenco.

Initially, the Albuquerque Festival was part of the anniversary celebration for the College of Fine Arts, and revenues from the performances were directed toward scholarships for Hispano students in the Theatre and Dance Department.[70] With little initial funding, producing the festival was no easy feat, but the spirit and love of flamenco brought out the best in everyone. Local artists in the first festival performed, lectured, and taught without compensation.[71] The event received accolades in all the local papers, including a review in the *Albuquerque Journal* that stated the first festival provided "a fitting and spectacular end to the 50th anniversary season of the University of New Mexico's College of Fine Arts," and went on to say, "The performance begins like an excited heartbeat as the 20 artists line the stage, clapping and stamping a steady rhythm. . . . This event proves that flamenco encompasses a variety of interpretations that keep it a rich living art."[72]

Posters for Festival Flamenco, Albuquerque, New Mexico.

A NEW GOLDEN ERA

As New Mexico experienced its golden era of flamenco dance and music, the popularity of flamenco was fading in the rest of the country. Large tours by José Greco, the company of Ximenez-Vargas, and others had almost come to a halt and would not be revived on a national scale until the arrival in 1983 of the companies of Antonio Gades and Mario Maya. Gades had previously come to the United States in 1969 and 1972 with long-time partner Cristina Hoyos. During the 1980s Gades and Maya took flamenco in directions not seen before, introducing it to a new audience that was mesmerized. The 1986 Broadway production *Flamenco Puro* (Pure Flamenco) put flamenco and Spanish dance back on the map, and flamenco once again became a household word. The show, which included the Montoya family from Spain, received widespread acclaim. That the Albuquerque Festival became a

Cristina Hoyos, Girona, Spain, c. 1965. Photograph by Colita.

respected and cherished event for students and the general public was due in part to the fact that Spanish dance had a history spanning at least fifty years in the state. However, its popularity also rode the wave of flamenco enthusiasm that came with *Flamenco Puro*.

Flamenco also reached new audiences through film. Even though the dance form had appeared in movies throughout the twentieth century, the 1980s saw the introduction of contemporary flamenco cinema via collaborations between top performers such as Gades and renowned film directors such as Carlos Saura. Rather than portraying the aflamencado style with Hollywood's flashy "Gypsy" dancers and

Antonio Gades, Girona, Spain, c. 1965. Photograph by Colita.
Gades and Hoyos reinvigorated the flamenco scene in Spain.
They collaborated on several film productions with Carlos Saura,
spreading the art form to new audiences around the world.

dangerous women, these films were artistic collaborations between practitioners
in the field who understood flamenco's history and where its future could lead.
Saura's 1981 film version of the theatrical production of Lorca's *Bodas de Sangre*
(Blood Wedding) starred Cristina Hoyos and Antonio Gades and featured his company. It was followed by the flamenco film version of Bizet's *Carmen* and a newly
staged all-flamenco version of *El Amor Brujo*. These films introduced the flamenco
tradition and culture to new generations of students. They also debuted theatrical

Poster for *Carmen: A Film by Carlos Saura*, 1983. This screen adaption of the famous opera used flamenco music and dance, which was interspersed with the classical score. The movie starred Antonio Gades and Laura del Sol, with Cristina Hoyos and Paco de Lucía.

innovations that allowed flamenco to break free of the constraints put into place during the Franco years.[73]

Throughout the 1990s both the Albuquerque Festival and Benítez's Teatro Flamenco continued to grow, attracting the best artists that Spain had to offer. Instead of students traveling to Spain, Spain came to New Mexico. Once again, collaboration and exchange flourished in the flamenco community. Artists often spent a summer season in Santa Fe and then returned to perform at the Albuquerque Festival. One such person was dancer and choreographer Pablo Rodarte. Of Mexican-American descent, Rodarte spent more than twenty years in Spain and touring the world in professional companies. Back in the United States, he was invited to join Benítez's company for a season and later performed at the Albuquerque Festival, receiving high acclaim. Enciñias-Sandoval asked him to join the UNM staff, and he taught flamenco and escuela bolera, which had never been done before. Rodarte also started a professional company, Dance España, and joined local groups, including Los Serranos. Professionals throughout the state admired Rodarte's talents as

above:
Eva Enciñias-Sandoval performs at Rodey Theatre on the UNM campus during the Festival Flamenco Internacional de Albuquerque, 1991. Photograph by Janet Borelli. Enciñias-Sandoval is wearing a *bata de cola* made from an antique *mantón de Manila* by dancer and designer Pablo Rodarte.

A performance by the Santa Fe-based flamenco group Los Serranos, c. 1992. *Left to right*: David Briggs (El Niño David) on guitar, Meg Savlov (Margarita) on vocals, Pablo Rodarte, and Susannah Garrett (Susana la Remolacha).

Costume sketch by dancer, choreographer, and costume
designer Pablo Rodarte, mid-1990s.

a choreographer, and one of his accomplishments was creating the holiday show
Navidad Flamenca, which toured the United States for several years.

During the 1990s Romero continued to collaborate on productions and tour
the United States. He performed in the first several years of the Albuquerque
Festival and taught some of the workshops. Tragically, in 1995 he died of a heart

attack after performing at the Joyce in New York, where he had shared billing with Benítez. Befitting Romero's energetic and giving nature, his final performance was an *alegría* (happiness), the most upbeat and energetic of all the flamenco genres. It was an appropriate end to an amazing career that was largely responsible for the flamenco scene in New Mexico. Many New Mexicans continue to credit him with their initiation into the techniques and nuances of flamenco and with kick-starting their careers.

Chapter 5

The Tradition Continues

Flamenco organizations such as María Benítez Teatro Flamenco and the Festival Flamenco Internacional de Albuquerque have proved their longevity and have surpassed their creators' most ambitious hopes and dreams. These and other programs have solidified New Mexico's international reputation as a center for flamenco. Great programming, continuing education, multiple generations of performers, teachers, and students, and the inclusion of both Spanish dance and traditional flamenco at local fiestas and fairs have all contributed to flamenco's place in the heart of New Mexico.

A LIVING LEGACY

In Albuquerque, Eva Enciñias-Sandoval passed the flamenco tradition down to her children, twins Joaquín and Marisol Enciñias. Both studied at an early age with their mother and their grandmother Clarita García de Aranda, and they began performing in Clarita's company at the age of five. They joined their mother's Ritmo Flamenco in their early teens, and both attended the dance program at the University of New Mexico, where they eventually became instructors. The Enciñias family and generations of other flamenco students have reaped the benefits of the artists who perform at the Albuquerque Festival, including both local performers

Dancer Alejandro Granados in a special appearance at Festival Flamenco Internacional de Albuquerque, 1993. Photograph by Janet Borelli.

opposite, top:
Marisol Enciñias performs a solo number at the Festival Flamenco, Albuquerque, New Mexico, c. mid-1990s. Photograph by Janet Borelli.

opposite, bottom:
Mother and son, Eva Enciñias-Sandoval (left) and Joaquín Enciñias, in a master class taught by guest artist Antonio Canales, who was brought from Seville, Spain, for the Festival Flamenco Internacional de Albuquerque, 1994. Photograph by Janet Borelli.

and out-of-town guests. Enciñias-Sandoval created a structure in which seasoned professionals not only star in the shows, but also conduct master classes. Even José Greco taught classes, and he also choreographed a special number for members of the university's performance group Alma Flamenca.

In 1999, with the Albuquerque Festival on solid ground, the Enciñias family branched out and began a new venture. Enciñias-Sandoval teamed up with Joaquín and Marisol to create the Conservatory of Flamenco Arts under the umbrella of the National Institute of Flamenco. The trio are co-directors of the conservatory, which is also home to the resident company Yjastros (Stepchildren): American Flamenco Repertory Company, an apt name since this showcases the dances of Spain even

International Flamenco star Antonio Canales in his US debut of *Torero* performed at Pope Joy Hall, Albuquerque, New Mexico, 1995. Photograph by Janet Borelli.

though the performers are not Spaniards. Joaquín Enciñias, who is the artistic director, choreographs the productions using innovative approaches to traditional forms. The institute brings in top professionals from Spain for special residencies and has commissioned several pieces for Yjastros. To date, the company has collected fifteen original flamenco choreographies from guest artists.[1] Marisol Enciñias, who received her MFA in dance from UNM in 2011, performs as a principal dancer in Yjastros. She also teaches at the university and serves as the artistic director for Alma Flamenca.

In the twenty-first century, Enciñias-Sandoval, Joaquín, and Marisol began selecting top performers from Madrid and the Bienal de Flamenco de Sevilla (Flamenco Biennial of Seville) to perform and teach at the Albuquerque Festival. More commonly referred to as the Seville Biennial, this event lasts for an entire month, bringing together the largest gathering of flamenco artists in the world. Top singers, musicians, and dancers perform in a concurso setting. Shows are produced at large theaters, historic landmarks, local bars and nightclubs, and small performance halls and are accompanied by special exhibitions of art and photography related to flamenco. After the Seville Biennial concludes, the stars travel to festivals around the world, such as the New York Flamenco Festival, held every March, and the Albuquerque Festival, held every June.

Dancer/choreographer Teo Morca with Carlos Menchaca and
Gretchen Williams, members of Yjastros: The American Flamenco
Repertory Company, in *El Museo*, Albuquerque, New Mexico, 2011.
Photo by Pat Barrett.

Tragically, in December 2013 the buildings housing the Conservatory of Flamenco Arts burned down, destroying costumes, music, archives, and business records. The Albuquerque community reached out in support, and dance studios around town lent their spaces for rehearsals and preparations for the 2014 festival. The twenty-seventh annual Albuquerque Festival went on, symbolizing the resilience of the New Mexican flamenco spirit. In an article in the *New York Daily News*, Marisol Enciñias stated, "We knew this festival would happen. . . . Flamenco is something that survives no matter what."[2] Later that year the organization opened in a new location, and guest residencies have continued at the university. In the fall of 2014, Antonio Canales returned to New Mexico for a six-week professorship. He had been one of the first Spanish stars to come to New Mexico and had debuted his theatrical production *Torero* (Bullfighter) at Popejoy Hall in 1995.

Students continue to flourish at the university. Three dancers, two of them now members of Yjastros, have received the prestigious Princess Grace Award for dance and performance. A former Yjastros member, Jesús Muñoz, opened his own studio in Albuquerque; he and dancer Valería Montes teach classes, produce concerts, and bring in guest artists for special workshops. During the summer of 2014 they began a bimonthly event called Tablao Flamenco, which is an informal juerga in which all of New Mexico's local artists are invited to join and share their knowledge.

María Benítez's legacy continues through her Institute for Spanish Arts in Santa Fe. In 2002 a resident company, Flamenco's Next Generation, was created to educate about, promote, and preserve the music and dance traditions of Spain. Benítez wanted to create something larger than simply a children's dance studio and to provide opportunities for growth and professional accomplishment. Flamenco's Next Generation is made up of local artists, many of whom grew up learning flamenco and Spanish classical dance at Benítez's institute. Members of Flamenco's Next Generation tour the state, perform at Santa Fe's annual Spanish Market and the Santa Fe Fiesta, and offer a six-week series of Sunday matinee performances at the Lodge at Santa Fe. Several students have traveled to Spain, and some have pursued careers in flamenco and Spanish dance. Others work with professionals from Spain who perform in Benítez's main company.

Several notable artists brought in by Benítez have chosen to reside in New Mexico. Others have created their own companies and return to perform in Santa Fe on their annual tours. Artists who stay in New Mexico create opportunities and partake of a flamenco scene that is collaborative, often innovative, and multigenerational. Several performers have worked for Benítez one season and then appeared the next season at the Albuquerque Festival. One such artist is guitarist José Valle Fajardo. Popularly known as "Chuscales," he was born to a Gypsy family in Granada, Spain, and learned to dance and later to play the guitar, performing in the Sacromonte cave La Golondrina, which was established by his grandparents in 1947.[3] While on tour in Canada he met María and Cecilio Benítez, who invited him to Santa Fe to

María Benítez on stage in Mississippi, c. mid-1990s.

Flamenco's Next Generation performs on the Santa Fe Plaza for the Twenty-Sixth Annual Spanish Market, 2013. *Left to right*: Simón Jaramillo, , Alex Martínez, Brianna Montijo. And at the Anderson Museum of Contemporary Art, Roswell, New Mexico, 2013. *Left to right*: Emmy Grimm (aka La Emi), Brianna Montijo, Alex Martínez, Simón Jaramillo, Jaylena Luján. Photograph by Art Tucker.

perform during the summer of 1988. Chuscales became the lead guitarist for María Benítez Teatro Flamenco, an artistic partnership that lasted almost two decades. He was invited by Enciñias-Sandoval to perform for the Albuquerque Festival, and he has appeared annually at that event ever since. He met his wife, Mina, originally from Tokyo, while on tour in New York. Originally trained in tap dancing in Japan, Mina Valle Fajardo switched to flamenco. The couple make Santa Fe their home, where Mina teaches locally and the two continue to perform together. When Chuscales is not on tour or involved in other engagements, he can be seen playing at local Santa Fe establishments such as El Mesón and Taberna la Boca or as a guest guitarist for Yjastros.[4]

Another performer brought in by Benítez is Juan Siddi. Of Spanish and Italian descent, Siddi grew up in Frankfurt, Germany, where he first encountered flamenco at local parties and juergas in the community of Spaniards residing in Germany. At age sixteen, Siddi moved to Barcelona, where an aunt lived, and began intensive flamenco studies. By eighteen he was dancing as a professional and touring the globe.[5] In 2002 he was invited by Benítez to be a principal dancer. After several seasons, Siddi, like Chuscales, made Santa Fe his home.

After nearly forty years of performing six nights a week and touring the globe, in 2009 Benítez retired and handed over the summer performances at the Lodge to Siddi, who not only danced as the soloist, but also took charge of all creative

Chuscales, Santa Fe, New Mexico, c. 1990s.
Photograph by Morgan Smith.

Juan Siddi, artistic director of Juan Siddi Flamenco Santa Fe, in his classic torero jacket performing his rendition of the *soleá*, Santa Fe, New Mexico, 2014. Photograph by Morgan Smith.

aspects, including choreography, lighting, and costume design. After the first summer season, which was well received by the community and the reviewers, Siddi took his company on a US tour that included a residency in San Francisco. When in Santa Fe, he taught flamenco at the studio of the Aspen Santa Fe Ballet. The year 2014 marked the beginning of a new venture for both Siddi and the ballet. With his five-year contract completed at the Lodge, Siddi's became the first resident flamenco company of the Aspen Santa Fe Ballet.[6] For its opening season, Juan Siddi Flamenco Santa Fe performed four shows at the Lensic Performing Arts Center. In the Santa Fe flamenco spirit, Siddi included an array of top professionals from Spain and the United States, especially New Mexico. His style is a combination of contemporary fusion, including piano and cello, and traditional flamenco.[7]

Another former principal dancer with Benítez has also returned to Santa Fe. Antonio Granjero grew up in Jerez de la Frontera, Spain, and began studying flamenco and classical Spanish dance at age ten. He toured as a child and in his teens with the Ballet Albarizuela and in 1991 moved to Madrid and performed with top artists. He joined Benítez Teatro Flamenco for twelve summer seasons. During Benítez's twentieth-anniversary season, the company included Estefanía Ramirez, a dancer who received her degree at UNM. After graduation Ramirez had moved

Estefanía Ramirez performing a guajira at the María Benítez
Cabaret, Santa Fe, New Mexico, 2014. Photo by Morgan Smith.

Antonio Granjero performing a soleá at the María Benítez
Cabaret, Santa Fe, New Mexico, 2014. Photo by Morgan Smith.

to Spain, where she toured and also taught. Granjero and Ramirez married and became co-directors of Entreflamenco, a company initially founded by Granjero in Spain. In 2011 the company was invited by Benítez for a month-long run in September, and these autumn performances continued through 2013. When Siddi's contract with the Lodge concluded, Benítez invited Granjero and Ramirez to head the 2014 summer season. Entreflamenco includes musicians and singers from Spain, but the core dancers are all New Mexicans who trained as children and teens with the Institute for Spanish Arts and at the university. Of their decision to hire an all–New Mexican cast, Ramirez said, "Of course we would not think otherwise about hiring dancers. We want to give back to the community in which we grew."[8] The Santa Fe community proved so welcoming and their first summer season was so successful that by the spring of 2015 the couple had moved to Santa Fe full time.

Other local artists who developed their craft at the institutes in Santa Fe and Albuquerque have also gone on to professional careers, spreading their love and passion for flamenco. Paco Antonio, formerly of Ritmo Flamenco, and Lucilene de Geus, who came to New Mexico as a dancer for Benítez, became dance partners

Paco Antonio and Lucilene de Geus, Las Cruces, New Mexico, c. 2000–2010. Photograph by Tim Jones.

and partners in life. They moved to Las Cruces in southern New Mexico, bringing the flamenco tradition with them. Antonio heads up the flamenco dance program at New Mexico State University, and de Geus teaches classes in flamenco, classical Spanish dance, and ballet. They also offer flamenco classes at local high schools. During the summers of 2013 and 2014, the couple conducted month-long trips to Spain, during which they arranged for students to attend master-training classes at the Amor de Dios studio in Madrid.[9]

Another performer who danced professionally with Benítez is Julia Chacón. Born in Albuquerque, she grew up in Phoenix, Arizona, where she was introduced as a teenager to flamenco and classical Spanish dance by Lydia Torea. A passionate student, Chacón attended the University of New Mexico with a double major in dance and anthropology. While in school she joined Campos and Castillo and their group, Rincón Flamenco, for several productions. Chacón studied at Madrid's prestigious Amor de Dios studio after graduating from college. Upon returning home,

Julia Chacón performs at the Crescent Ballroom, Phoenix, Arizona, 2014. Photograph by Mary Nellie Brown.

she was hired to perform in Benítez's company, staying for four seasons. Chacón eventually moved to Santa Fe full time and created her own company, Inspiración Flamenca. The group often performs on Sunday evenings at Taberna la Boca. Chacón now divides her time between Phoenix and Santa Fe and also continues studying and performing in Spain.[10]

Many of the young performers who participated in flamenco's birth in New Mexico during the 1960s and 1970s are still active as guest teachers and choreographers; they produce lectures and demonstrations about the history of flamenco; and they serve on discussion panels for the flamenco community and in the larger milieu of art and culture. Castillo, who retired from flamenco in 1993, continued for another seventeen years as a performer and choreographer of classical Spanish dance for opera companies throughout the United States. Campos continues to teach guitar and performs regularly, collaborating with New Mexican folk and jazz musicians, as well as flamencos. In June 2014 the couple celebrated their fiftieth wedding anniversary—and were it not for flamenco and Vicente Romero,

Lili del Castillo and the full cast of the Tulsa Opera, Oklahoma, c. 2005.

Luís Campos in a performance at Teatro Paraguas, Santa Fe, New Mexico, 2010. Photograph by Andrew John Cecil.

David Briggs (El Niño David) in a performance at Teatro Paraguas, Santa Fe, New Mexico, 2010. Photograph by Andrew John Cecil.

they might not have met. Morca still resides in Taos today, using it as a home base. He is in demand as a teacher and choreographer, and he lectures on the history of flamenco and his personal experiences. He also produces handmade castanets, a traditional craft he learned in Spain. Briggs, who arrived as a student and aficionado at the height of the El Nido and La Zambra days, received a PhD in Spanish literature and is currently a professor of Spanish at the University of New Mexico and Santa Fe Community College, where he teaches popular classes on flamenco. Rodarte is currently employed at the University of Arizona in Tucson in the theater department. He also continues to teach, perform, and work as a choreographer.

In 2012, a multigenerational collaboration began between Teo Morca, Carlos Lomas, and Vicente Griego. Lomas and Morca, of course, have been a part of New Mexico's flamenco scene for years. Griego, a native New Mexican who grew up in the town of Dixon, was first exposed to flamenco during childhood. He studied flamenco cante and is now the lead singer for Yjastros. When not performing with Yjastros, he tours with other companies and lectures on the history and structure

Guitarist Carlos Lomas, singer Vicente Griego (left), and dancer Teo
Morca join together for a week long Flamenco intensive workshop in
Missoula, Montana, 2014. Photograph by Victoria Lenihan.

of flamenco cante. In September 2012, Lomas and Morca invited Griego to partici-
pate in the first four-day flamenco festival in Missoula, Montana. It met with an
enthusiastic flamenco community, and the festival was repeated in September 2013
and 2014. In their third season, they offered lessons in guitar, cante, and dance
(accompanied by guitar and cante), with a concentration on structure and how the
different aspects of flamenco fit together. In New Mexico, the three present lectures
in urban and rural communities, at schools, and at other public institutions.[11]

Nearly fifty-five years after the introduction of traditional flamenco by Vicente
Romero, the wide variety of programs throughout New Mexico is evidence that
flamenco is a prominent part of the state's identity. As of the writing of this book,
the Albuquerque Festival is preparing for its twenty-eighth year, which will include
more than thirty workshops. The UNM Dance Department is a major destination
for students who wish to concentrate on flamenco. The Institute for Spanish Arts
is going strong. Sadly, during the spring of 2014, one of the community's founders,
Cecilio Benítez, passed away. Flamenco's Next Generation dedicated its summer
season to his memory, emphasizing that his legacy continues. María Benítez credits
him for her success: "If it weren't for Cecilio pushing me to go forward, I might

have spent my entire career going from company to company. . . . I never would have thought back then that we would accomplish everything we have now."[12] She still calls Santa Fe home, plays an active role in the direction of the organization, and finds time to teach multiple generations of students.

Echoing the thriving days of years gone by, on any given night during the summer season in Santa Fe, tourists and locals can choose between several performances by New Mexico's talented companies. El Farol, a historic landmark for flamenco performance, is the summer home of Yjastros, which performs six nights a week. Several restaurants hold monthly or biweekly flamenco nights. El Mesón hosts the group Flamenco Conpaz, which features former Next Generation dancer Domino Martínez; Chuscales and Mina; and guitarist Joaquín Gallegos of Santa Fe, who as a child began his studies with Carlos Lomas. Chuscales and Gallegos also play solo shows at Taberna on a regular basis. Taos dancer Catalina Rio-Fernández brings in guest artists from Spain and performs at local establishments in Santa Fe and at festivals throughout the state.

Guitarist Joaquín Gallegos and dancer Carlos Menchaca perform a *soleá* at Skylight Bar, Santa Fe, New Mexico, 2015. Photograph by Morgan Smith.

Dancer La Emi performs in a *martinete* sung by Vicente Griego at Skylight
Bar, Santa Fe, New Mexico, 2015. Photograph by Morgan Smith.

AROUND THE WORLD AND BACK

Flamenco's acceptance as an integral part of New Mexican culture can be
directly attributed to the dedicated dancers, vocalists, musicians, and educators who
have pursued it as both a passion and a profession. Its success is also a result of the
worldwide exploration and embracing of flamenco as a vibrant, living art form. In
Spain the tradition continues in family settings, local ferias and fiestas, and theatrical performance venues. It is still handed down from generation to generation in
close-knit communities, but it is also taught in academies throughout the country.

The field of flamencology, which includes the art form's history, anthropology,
and ethnomusicology, is rapidly expanding at universities and research centers,
which have developed archives that document the history and development of
flamenco over the centuries. The oldest of these institutions is the Centro Andaluz
de Documentación del Flamenco (Andalusian Center for Flamenco Documenta-
tion), which opened its doors nearly twenty years ago in Jerez de la Frontera. As the
leading research facility dedicated to the history of flamenco in all forms—dance,
music, and cante—the center contains an archive of historical documents, ephemera, and obscure musical recordings. More recently, three entities dedicated to flamenco opened in Seville: the Instituto Andaluz del Flamenco (Andalusian Institute

of Flamenco), the Museo del Baile Flamenco (Museum of Flamenco Dance), and the Casa de la Memoria (House of Memory). The Instituto Andaluz del Flamenco opened in 2005 to promote knowledge of flamenco and to maintain flamenco as a living tradition. The institute presents exhibitions on flamenco history and about specific performers of the past, and it is home to a company called Ballet Flamenco de Andalucía. The Museo del Baile Flamenco, which was opened in 2006 by dancer Cristina Hoyos, houses an interactive exhibition space, art galleries, class-rooms, and a small theater for nightly performances. The Casa de la Memoria, which opened in 2002, specializes in the presentation of exhibitions, courses, and conferences dedicated to preserving flamenco from the café cantante era. Dancers also perform live in the exhibition space, reprising dances and sequences made famous by earlier performers.

Perhaps the most significant recognition of flamenco as a cultural tradition was the 2010 announcement by the United Nations Educational, Scientific, and Cultural Organization proclaiming flamenco to be an "intangible cultural heritage in need of urgent safeguarding." Funding poured in from regional and local governmental agencies in support of flamenco institutions and their collaborations with entities outside Andalusia, including cross-programming with countries such as the United States. In 2012, Seville designated Albuquerque, New Mexico, as a sister city because of the preservation and promotion of flamenco at the Festival Flamenco Internacional de Albuquerque, which is among the largest concursos around the globe. While the Seville Biennial remains the largest and is one of the oldest gatherings, aficionados need not travel to Spain to witness a wide array of theatrical flamenco. Flamenco gatherings now happen in North America, South America, Denmark, France, Japan, and other locales internationally.

Japan embraced flamenco almost as enthusiastically as New Mexico did, and the timeline there parallels that of the United States. Japan's introduction to traditional flamenco came with the appearance of La Argentina in 1929. The company of Ximenez-Vargas performed in 1955, and Pilar López brought her troupe in 1960. The national godmother of flamenco, Yoko Komatsubara, contributed to the field much in the same manner as Vicente Romero and María Benítez, and Komatsubara is one of the few non-Spaniards to bring her company to the Seville Biennial. Today, Japan has the largest flamenco population outside Spain, with nearly 80,000 students attending the country's 600 Spanish dance academies.[13] Dancers from New Mexico who studied in Spain recall that Japanese students outnumbered all other nationalities besides Spanish. New Mexico's connection with Japan includes Mina Valle Fajardo, who performed at Juan Isshiki's flamenco tablao, one of the oldest in Tokyo.[14]

In the twenty-first century, New Mexicans and students from around the world continue to study dance and music in the academies of Spain, keeping them alive. Private lessons in the homes of Spain's individual guitarists, singers, and dancers also thrive due to the influx of both local and international students. When the

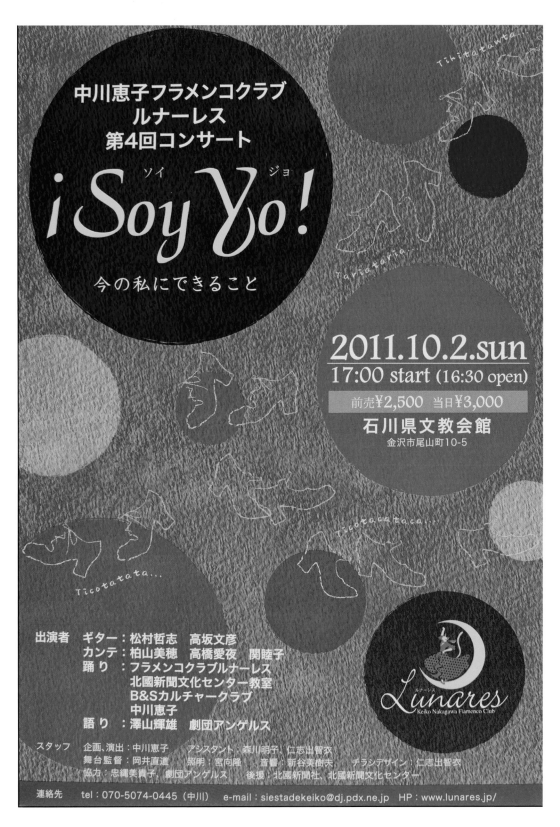

Poster announcing flamenco show, Kanazawa, Japan, 2011.

Mantón by Katsuta Shinpyo, Suzu, Japan, 2001. Ink and watercolor on Japanese paper, 37 ⅖ x 23 ⅗ in. The artist traveled to Spain and was enthralled with flamenco music and dance. He painted a flamenco series that was displayed at the Prefectural Museum of Art in Kanazawa, Japan, August 2013.

Bata de cola and Noh mask by Hawhiko Okuhama, Tokyo, Japan, 2013. This Tokyo-based artist is involved in both flamenco and Japanese Noh theater. He expertly blends the two traditions by creating exquisite contemporary costumes using recycled wedding kimonos. Photograph by Hori.

Juan del Gastor, a guitarist descended from a long line of Gitano performers, and students from Japan and the United States practice flamenco in a *juerga*-style setting on a hot summer night in Seville, Spain, June 2013. Photograph by author.

professional artists go on tour, it is often their advanced students who take over local performances. This includes New Mexicans, many of whom get their early performing experiences while studying in Spain. When they return to New Mexico, they bring with them an encyclopedia of flamenco knowledge to share.

In New Mexico, protégés of the state's flamenco pioneers are now in their prime, studying, teaching, researching, and performing on a regular basis. The next generation of young flamencologists, ethnomusicologists, folklorists, dance historians, and performers are entering universities, where they continue the tradition of enhancing and contributing to the growth of the community.

The twenty-first century also has seen the return of flamenco-themed juergas and sevillanas jams. These parties are often set up like Andalusian ferias, and the participants dress in feria costumes and sing and dance all evening, recalling the old days in Spain or the early years at El Nido. They tie the past to the present while looking toward the future, since many of the participants are the students of the first and second generation of flamencos in New Mexico. In this way, flamenco has become a multigenerational tradition in New Mexico, handed down from teacher to

The author (facing) with dancer Leisa Forman of Santa Fe at a *sevillanas* jam, Neptune Gallery, Santa Fe, New Mexico, 2011.

student, parent to child, and cousin to cousin. When the summer flamenco performance season closes, locals still gather to play their guitars and dance flamenco. In its many manifestations, flamenco in New Mexico is here to stay.

Acknowledgments

A project of this magnitude would not have been possible without the support and encouragement of many individuals. Words alone cannot show the depth of my gratitude, which would best be expressed in *flamenco cante* (song) and sharing a good glass of *jerez* (sherry). First and foremost, I wish to thank Marsha C. Bol, PhD, director of twhe Museum of International Folk Art, for the opportunity to put my passion and enthusiasm for all things flamenco to good use. The exhibition and this book would not have been possible without her encouragement and the support of the International Folk Art Foundation and the Museum of New Mexico Foundation. Museum volunteers Dan Prall, Marlene Lind, Cheryl Roth, Ava Fullerton, and Barbara Forslund assisted during photo shoots of museum objects. Barbara Windom generously provided her beautiful space, expert trainers Roberto Quijandría and Lucho Depleo, and award-winning horses at La Estancia Alegre in Alcalde, New Mexico. Thanks to Maureen Russell, museum conservator, for the introduction. Photographer Blair Clark devoted hours and worked on-site at the museum and off at Estancia Alegre, ensuring the completion of catalog images.

My dance parents, Lili del Castillo and Luís Campos, have given years of themselves, sharing their love and passion for all things flamenco, including hours in the studio and at performances, analyzing, comparing notes, enjoying music, meals, and laughter. Dr. David Briggs, often referred to by his students as "the best Spanish teacher ever," is my living, breathing flamenco encyclopedia. María Benítez, dancer extraordinaire, provided her guidance and knowledge during my tenure in her Segunda Compañia and beyond. Eva Enciñías-Sandoval welcomed me into her group Alma Flamenca while I was a student at the University of New Mexico and served as a reader on my master's thesis, "Women of the Guadalquivir: Female Flamenco Singers (1880-1936)." Pablo Rodarte taught me the intricacies of Spanish classical dance and *escuela bolera* and also shared his personal stories. Teo Morca is an inspiration for his talent, *charlas* (in-depth conversations), and great coffee. Ana Börger-Greco welcomed me into her home and allowed full access to the costume collection of the late José Greco. Exhibition designer Nancy Allen put me in contact with Ana Börger-Greco. Elizabeth Serna Cárdenas, Theresa Cárdenas, and Vivian and Pedro Cuadra also welcomed me into their homes, sharing their personal archives and flamenco stories. Many others in the local flamenco community contributed to this project in one way or another, including Miguel Romero, José Valle Fajardo "Chuscales," Carlos Lomas, Giovanna Brandi, Julia Chacón, Lydia Torea, Emi Grimm, Morgan Smith, and Janet Borelli. Many who are not named here are included in this book and exhibition, and I hope they pay proper tribute.

Field research in Spain and Japan was made less difficult and quite pleasurable by dear friends and local consultants. Remedios Guillén sought out and drove me to obscure locations or neighborhoods nearby in search of objects for the exhibition and also provided historical family photos for research. Genoveva Enriquez and the *familia* García Gughieri allowed me into their private world at the *feria de abril* in Seville. Jesús Muñusuri Sanz acted as a local tour guide, translator, and locator of rare posters seen in shop windows. Guitarist Juan Carlos Berlanga, whom I first met when he joined María Benítez for a summer season in Santa Fe, has been a constant provider of information on all things flamenco and shared contacts in both Spain and Japan, where he toured regularly. Marina Alfonso Mola and Carlos Martínez Shaw were fabulous hosts, opening up their home for extended stays. My friend and colleague Daisuke Murata was instrumental in translating Japanese flamenco posters into English, locating artists, and driving me to obscure flamenco studios in Kanazawa, Japan. Mina Fajardo and Ayumi Kitajima provided contact information for local flamencos in Tokyo and introduced me to Tokyo's oldest flamenco establishment, *El Flamenco*. Haruhiko Okuhama, flamenco dancer and costume designer, kindly welcomed me into his studio and helped me get onto the proper subway back to my hotel. Yuriko Saga drove me through many Tokyo neighborhoods in search of Okuhama's studio.

Most important is the love, inspiration, and encouragement I have received and continue to receive from my family. My grandparents, Antonio E. and Marilyn S. Chávez, first introduced me to flamenco and Spanish culture as a child. My parents, Thomas E. Chávez and Jennifer Francis, provided the opportunity to take my first dance lessons and drove me to and from classes, rehearsals, and shows. They and my stepparents, Celia López-Chávez and John Francis, have provided continued support and encouragement through college, graduate school, and my current career at the museum. My children Noé Antonio and Alexina Christel García Chávez, fifteenth-generation New Mexicans, carry on our family traditions and are my continued inspiration every day. They have attended many performances, lectures, and demonstrations on flamenco and have also accompanied me more than once to the Museo del Baile Flamenco in Seville, Spain, where they provided much -needed feedback from the point of view of our next generation of museum-goers and art and history buffs.

Notes

PREFACE

1. Interview with Miguel Romero, Santa Fe, NM, April 22, 2014.

CHAPTER 1

1. For a description of the four dance families of Spain, see Matteo, *Language of Spanish Dance*. Another description of the four genres by dancer-choreographer Teodoro Morca does not include *estilo Andaluz* as a separate genre but rather includes it in the family of regional dances. As a fourth genre, Morca includes contemporary theatrical dance. See Morca, *Becoming the Dance*, 64–65.

2. For a good discussion in English on the origins of flamenco songs, see Matteo, *Language of Spanish Dance*; and Pohren, *Art of Flamenco*. In Spain, many flamencologists have studied the genealogy of flamenco song; see Blas Vega and Ríos Ruiz, *Diccionario Enciclopédico Ilustrado del Flamenco*; and Ríos Ruiz, *El Gran Libro del Flamenco*; and Machado y Alvarez, *Colección de cantes flamencos*.

3. Throughout the text, I have chosen to capitalize the words Gitano and Gypsy since they refer to a specific group of people inside Spain. I am not referring to the larger group that has spread around the world.

4. The term *flamenco* can be used to describe the art form itself or it can be used to describe a person who is dedicated to flamenco. Since it is a Spanish term, it is gender-specific. For example, a group of people in the flamenco community are referred to as *flamencos*. If that group is made up of only women, they are referred to as *flamencas*.

5. Serra, "Traditional Costumes of Spain," 75.

6. These common jaleos translate as "well done," "beautiful," "that's how you dance it," and "that's how you play it." The term *olé* has no direct translation, although one theory says that it is derived from the word Allah, implying "from God." The term is shouted when the movements or music seem to flow out of the performer as if by divine force.

7. *Cantaora* is the female form of the term for a flamenco singer. The male counterpart is *cantaor*. The plural forms are *cantaoras* and *cantaores*.

8. López Moya, *Pastora Imperio*, 38. This is the earliest known biography of Pastora Imperio and is an in-depth look at the life of a young star who bridged the gap between the café cantante era, the variedades, and classical theater.

9. Jaime Phissa in *Poesía*, 107. See also interview with Manuel de Falla by Rafael Benedito in *La Patria* (Madrid, April 15, 1915); Falla describes his admiration for both Pastora Imperio and Rosario Monje.

10. Blake, "A Certain Comb, a Certain Shawl, a Certain Flower." See also Pritchard, *Diaghilev and the Ballets Russes*. This exhibition catalog contains several scholarly essays related to Diaghilev's collaborations with the avant-garde and his time in Spain. Of particular interest are Jane Pritchard, "Creating Productions"; John E. Bowlt, "Léon Bakst, Natalia Goncharova and Pablo Picasso"; and Juliet Bellow, "When Art Danced with Music."

11. There is no direct translation for the term *cuadro flamenco*. It loosely translates as flamenco quartet; however, it generally refers to any flamenco group, no matter how large or small.

12. Pineda Novo, *Juana la Macarrona*, 44–45. Juana la Macarrona was considered one of the greatest dancers of the café cantante era. She performed in the show *Cuadro Flamenco* with her partner Ramirez, dancer María Albaicín, and cantaora La Rubia de Jerez.

13. There are many books on the works of Federico García Lorca and Manuel de Falla and their involvement in the Primer Concurso del Cante Jondo. See, for example, Persia, *I Concurso de Cante Jondo*; and Molina Fajardo, *Manuel de Falla y el Cante Jondo*.

14. Triana, *Arte y Artistas Flamencos* (1935), 158–159. Fernando de Triana had such appreciation and admiration for La Argentina that he dedicated his book to her, calling her the "messenger dove for the art of flamenco." See also Escudero, *Mi Baile*; García Redondo, *El Círculo Mágico*.

15. Recordings of these songs can be heard on the digitally remastered album *Colección de Canciones Populares Españolas: Federico García Lorca (piano), La Argentinita (voz)* (Sonifolk, 1994).

16. The poem was written between 1921 and 1924 but not published until 1927 or 1928. It depicts a rivalry between two brothers outside the famous café cantante of the same name in Málaga, Spain. The café cantante was open from 1857 to 1937. Several flamenco tablaos today carry the same name.

17. For an early biography of Encarnación López at the beginning of her career, see López Moya, *La Argentinita*. For descriptions of her collaborative efforts and theatrical works, see Novo, *Juana la Macarrona*; Woodall, *In Search of the Firedance*; and Puig-Claramunt and Albaicín, *El Arte del Baile Flamenco*.

18. Interview with Vivian Cuadra, Albuquerque, NM, January 12, 2008; interview with Lili del Castillo, Albuquerque, NM, December 31, 2007; interview with María Benítez, Santa Fe, NM, August 2, 2014.

19. Pack, *Tourism and Dictatorship*.

CHAPTER 2

1. Kagan, "The Spanish Craze."

2. Payne, "The Reencounter between the United States and Spain."

3. Morca, *Becoming the Dance*, 121; Bennahum and Goldberg, *100 Years of Flamenco in New York*.

4. Bennahum, "Gypsy Bodies/Images of Carmen."

5. Kagan, "The Spanish Craze," 32; and Labanyi, "The American Connection."

6. Bennahum, *Antonia Mercé*, 186–194.

7. Fernández, "Poets, Peasants, Painters, Professors and Performers in New York."

8. Bennahum, *Antonia Mercé*, 183–195. This section of Bennahum's biography on La Argentina provides a detailed timeline of all her shows and tours between 1905 and 1936.

9. An exhibition of Escudero's paintings was hosted at the Museo del Baile Flamenco. See the exhibition catalog Museo del Baile Flamenco, *Vicente Escudero*. For a description of his philosophy and multidisciplinary approach, see his biography, *Mi Baile*.

10. Ríos Ruiz, *El Gran Libro del Flamenco*, 248–250.

11. News tidbits announcing the dedication of the bronze sculpture of La Argentina are in *American Dancer* (February 1949): 8.

12. Draegin, "Fanning the Spanish Fever." Interview with Teo Morca, Taos, NM, August 2011; interview with Lili del Castillo and Luís Campos, Albuquerque, NM, December 31, 2007; interview with María Benítez, Santa Fe, NM, August 2, 2014.

13. Zatanía-Rios, "100 Years of Carmen Amaya."

14. Ibid.

15. Ibid.

16. Morca, *Becoming the Dance*, 123.

17. Ibid., 64–65.

18. Interviews with Teo Morca, Taos, NM, May 2010 and August 2011. See also Morca, *Becoming the Dance*, 1–3.

19. Torea and Bezunartea, *La Gitana Blanca*, 26–30.

20. Interviews with Betty Serna Cárdenas, Albuquerque, NM, December 19, 2013, and February 12, 2014.

21. "Spanish Dancer from Brooklyn."

22. "Versatile Latin American," 7.

23. Ibid. Many other articles also discuss Greco's discovery by La Argentinita; for a full overview of Greco's life and work, see his autobiography, *The Gypsy in My Soul*.

24. "Versatile Latin American."

25. Williams, "Iberia in London 3," 14.

26. Greene, "Greco Dance Group Clicks."

27. Swan, "Greco and Troupe Perform."

28. Interview with David Briggs, Santa Fe, New Mexico, April 15, 2014.

29. Torea and Bezunartea, *La Gitana Blanca*, 142.

30. Thomas, "Always Searching for Beautiful Talent."

31. Ibid.

32. Labanyi, "The American Connection," 92, 111.

1. Cadena Sur/Radio Sevilla, *150 Años de Feria en Sevilla*, 2. An early description of costumes at the feria was given by a man named Nicolás Salas.

2. Ybarra's original description appears in Cadena Sur/Radio Sevilla, *150 Años de Feria en Sevilla*, 1.

3. For more on this time period, including the Spain Is Different campaign and the government's support of Festivales de España, see Pack, *Tourism and Dictatorship*.

4. For information on SIMOF and recordings of previous runway shows, see http://www.simof.es. Reviews of the shows and video can be found at http://www.flamenco-world.com.

5. Kagan, "The Spanish Craze," 25–30.

6. McCracken, *The Life and Writing of Fray Angélico Chávez*, 10–12. Conversation with Thomas E. Chávez, August 9, 2014. Chávez's grandfather Fabian Chávez and grand-uncle Gustavo Sosaya worked on the re-creation of the San Estevan Mission in San Diego. The buildings are now part of Balboa Park.

7. Kagan, "The Spanish Craze," 25–30.

8. During the Pueblo Revolt, several Native tribes banded together, revolted against the colonizers, and threw the Spanish out. It was the earliest successful revolution on American soil. The Spanish returned thirteen years later, along with Native American allies, and reentered New Mexican territory.

9. The statue of La Conquistadora is the oldest European image of the Madonna in the United States. She was first brought to Santa Fe's Church of the Assumption in 1625. She was taken out of New Mexico with the fleeing Spanish colonists during the Pueblo Revolt of 1680 and then returned to Santa Fe with Vargas in 1693. Fray Angélico Chávez, "Our Lady of the Conquest," 18–29. Chávez also wrote a biographical novel about the virgin: Chávez, *The Lady from Toledo*.

10. For an in-depth look at the history of the Santa Fe Fiesta and its various components, see Pierce, *Que Vivan las Fiestas*. This volume of essays accompanied an exhibition by the same name at the Museum of International Folk Art in 1985.

11. Chávez, "Santa Fe's Own: A History of Fiesta," 7–10.

12. "Music and the Fiesta."

13. "Friday Night Entertainment at La Fonda."

14. For a discussion of traditional fiesta fashion, see Fisher, "Costume Equals Festive Fiesta."

15. Interview with Monica Sosaya Halford, Santa Fe, NM, September 10, 2010.

16. Interviews with Betty Serna Cárdenas, Albuquerque, NM, December 19, 2013, and February 12, 2014. See also Pacheco, "Life Filled with Dance."

17. "Flamenco Group Performs at Museum"; "Flamenco Spotlighted at Fiesta"; and "Miguel Galvez to Sing Flamenco at Folk Art."

18. "Fiesta Is a Big Event"; "Flamenco for Culture."

19. "Kicking Up Her Heels."

20. Interview with María Benítez, Santa Fe, NM, August 2, 2014.

CHAPTER 4

1. *La Gitana Studio of Dancing Mid-Term Recital.*

2. Interview with Vivian Cuadra, Albuquerque, NM, January 12, 2008.

3. Interview with Betty Serna Cárdenas, Albuquerque, NM, February 12, 2014.

4. Ibid.

5. Pacheco, "Life Filled with Dance."

6. Interviews with Lili del Castillo, Albuquerque, NM, December 31, 2007, and February 11, 2014.

7. Interview with Lili del Castillo, Albuquerque, NM, December 31, 2007.

8. Interview with Vivian Cuadra, Albuquerque, NM, January 12, 2008.

9. "Tiny Señoritas Wow <AP>Em"; interviews with Lili del Castillo, Albuquerque, NM, December 31, 2007, and February 9, 2014; interviews with Vivian Cuadra, January 12, 2008, and September 5, 2014.

10. Interview with Vivian Cuadra and Pedro Cuadra, Albuquerque, NM, January 12, 2008.

11. Interview with Luís Campos, Albuquerque, NM, February 9, 2014.

12. Interview with Luís Campos, Albuquerque, NM, December 31, 2007.

13. W. B., "Romero Olé," 37.

14. Interview with Vivian Cuadra, Albuquerque, NM, January 12, 2008; *New Mexico Magazine* (1957), clipping in collection of Vivian Cuadra; see also de Baca, "Olé Vicente."

15. Artist biography in *Guitar, Lorca, and Flamenco.*

16. Ibid.

17. Ibid.

18. Thompson, "Romero Show Gets Hand."

19. "Superb Spanish Dance Set Today at St. John's."

20. Interview with Miguel Romero, Santa Fe, NM, April 22, 2014; *El Nido's Patio Flamenco Presents June through August Annually Vicente Romero and His Cuadro Flamenco.*

21. "Traditional Spanish Flamenco to Open in Santa Fe."

22. "Talk of the Area."

23. "Local Boy Makes Good." This article announced Romero's anticipated appearance on the show. An image of Romero with Garson and Linkletter appeared in a subsequent article, "A Benefit Performance."

24. Dohme, "Real Flamenco Hits Santa Fe."

25. Ibid.

26. "Traditional Spanish Flamenco to Open in Santa Fe."

27. "Flamenco Group Performs at Museum"; and "Flamenco Spotlighted at Fiesta."

28. "Vicente Romero Concert Set by LA Opera Guild."

29. Unidentified newspaper article in Vivian Cuadra's collection.

30. Conversation with Miguel Romero, Santa Fe, NM, April 22, 2014.

31. "Miguel Galvez to Sing Flamenco at Folk Art."

32. Interview with David Briggs, Albuquerque, NM, January 11, 2008.

33. Murphy, "Ruben Romero's Gypsy Soul."

34. "Miguel Galvez to Sing Flamenco at Folk Art."

35. "Romero Envisions State Dance Tour."

36. Conversation with David Briggs, Santa Fe, NM, April 15, 2014.

37. Interview with Teo Morca, Taos, NM, August 15, 2011. See also Morca, *Becoming the Dance*, 126–128.

38. Interview with María Benítez, Santa Fe, NM, August 2, 2014. See also Pikula, "María Benítez"; and King, "The Two Sides of María Benítez."

39. Interview with María Benítez, Santa Fe, NM, August 2, 2014.

40. Ibid.

41. Ibid. See also King, "The Two Sides of María Benítez"; and Pikula, "María Benítez."

42. Interview with María Benítez, Santa Fe, NM, August 2, 2014.

43. W. B., "Romero Olé."

44. Conversation with David Briggs, Santa Fe, NM, April 15, 2014.

45. Jorge Midon quoted in unidentified clipping, c. June 1971, found in scrapbook of Jean Critchfield.

46. *La Zambra de Santa Fe, Restaurante-Tablao Flamenco.*

47. Newspaper advertisement in scrapbook of Jean Critchfield.

48. Interview with María Benítez, Santa Fe, NM, August 2, 2014.

49. Ibid.

50. Vural, "The Mother of New Mexico Flamenco."

51. Pikula, "María Benítez," 50.

52. Campbell, "With María Benítez in Santa Fe," 9.

53. Graebner, "*Feria* Needs Change."

54. Interview with Lili del Castillo and Luís Campos, February 9, 2014.

55. Nolan, "Teo Morca"; interview with Teo Morca, Taos, NM, May 8, 2008.

56. *Los Alamos Arts Council Presents Estampa Flamenca.*

57. Conversation with David Briggs, Santa Fe, NM, April 15, 2014.

58. Conversation with David Briggs, Santa Fe, NM, July 20, 2014.

59. Interview with Carlos Lomas, Santa Fe, NM, August 22, 2014.

60. Ibid.

61. Pikula, "María Benítez."

62. Rosen, "María Benítez Spanish Dance Company."

63. Bialor, "The José Greco Company," 31.

64. Bialor, "María Benítez Spanish Dance Company."

65. "Flamenco Dance Festival Slated at UNM."

66. "Olions Sponsor Ritmo Flamenco Show at Civic."

67. Ibid.

68. Interview with Teo Morca, Taos, NM, August, 15, 2011.

69. Interviews with Lili del Castillo, December 31, 2007, and February 9, 2014.

70. "Flamenco Dance Festival Slated at UNM"; "Flamenco <AP>87."

71. Mazur, "Festival Flamenco Stamps in Triumph."

72. Ibid.

73. For a discussion and critique of Gades's and Saura's collaborative efforts on film, see Hayes, *Flamenco*.

CHAPTER 5

1. *Festival Flamenco Internacional de Albuquerque.*

2. "New Mexico Flamenco Festival Rises from the Ashes."

3. Interview with José and Mina Valle Fajardo, Santa Fe, NM, April 5, 2014; García, "Cave of Creativity." For a history of the caves of the Sacromonte in Granada and Fajardo's relatives, see Albaicín, *Zambras de Granada y Flamencos del Sacromonte.*

4. Interview with José and Mina Valle Fajardo, Santa Fe, NM, April 5, 2014.

5. June, "I Am Flamenco."

6. Aspen Santa Fe Ballet, "Juan Siddi Flamenco Santa Fe Finds New Footing with Aspen Santa Fe Ballet."

7. "Juan Siddi Flamenco Santa Fe," *Santa Fean Now: The City of Santa Fe Event Calendar,* July 17, 2014, 15; Smith, "Mind, Body, Soles."

8. Conversation with Estefanía Ramirez, Santa Fe, NM, August 10, 2014. For the 2014 season Entreflamenco's company included Alice Blumenfeld of Albuquerque, Miquela Wiegel of Santa Fe, and Keyana Deaguero of Española. See also Simpson, "Power Spot: Flamenco in Santa Fe."

9. Conversation with Paco Antonio and Lucilene de Geus, Santa Fe, NM, July 18, 2014.

10. Conversation with Julia Chacón, Seville, Spain, June 22, 2013. See also Snyder, "Hear the Heartbeat"; and http://www.juliachacon.com.

11. Interview with Carlos Lomas, Santa Fe, NM, August 22, 2014.

12. Interview with María Benítez, Santa Fe, NM, August 2, 2014.

13. Shikaze, "Flamenco in Japan"; see also Elson, "Flamenco Continues to Take Japan by Storm"; and Gulati, "Far East Flamenco."

14. Interview with Mina Valle Fajardo, April 5, 2014.

Bibliography

Albaicín, Curro. *Zambras de Granada y Flamencos del Sacromonte: Una Historia Flamenco en Granada*. Córdoba, Spain: Almuzara, 2011.

Aspen Santa Fe Ballet. "Juan Siddi Flamenco Santa Fe Finds New Footing with Aspen Santa Fe Ballet." April 18, 2014, http://www.aspensantafeballet.com/juan-siddi/juan-siddi-article.html (accessed August 23, 2014).

"A Benefit Performance." *Santa Fe New Mexican*, May 8, 1966.

Bennahum, Ninotchka Devorah. *Antonia Mercé, "La Argentina": Flamenco and the Spanish Avant-Garde*. Hanover, NH: University Press of New England, 2000.

———. "Gypsy Bodies/Images of Carmen." Paper presented at the 5th Biennial New Perspectives in Flamenco: History and Research Symposium, Albuquerque, NM, June 8–9, 2014.

Bennahum, Ninotchka, and K. Meira Goldberg. *100 Years of Flamenco in New York*. New York: New York Public Library for the Performing Arts, 2013.

Bialor, Perry. "The José Greco Company, Jan. 30–Feb. 18, 1990." *Attitude: The Dancers' Monthly* 16, no. 3 (Spring 1990): 31.

———. "María Benítez Spanish Dance Company, December 12–24, 1989." *Attitude: The Dancers' Monthly* 6, no. 3 (Spring 1990): 31.

Blake, Jody. "A Certain Comb, a Certain Shawl, a Certain Flower: Natalia Goncharova's Spanish Dancers." In *The Spanish Night: Flamenco, Avant-Garde and Popular Culture 1865–1936*, ed. Patricia Molins and Pedro G. Romero, 143–159. Madrid: Museo Nacional Centro de Arte Reina Sofía, 2008.

Blas Vega, José. *Los Cafés Cantantes de Madrid*. Madrid: Guillermo Blásquez, 2006.

———. *Los Cafés Cantantes de Sevilla*. Barcelona: Cinterco, 1987.

———. *Conversaciones Flamencos con Aurelio de Cádiz*. Madrid: Librería Valle, 1978.

———. *Vida y Cante de Don Antonio Chacón: La Edad de Oro del Flamenco (1869–1929)*. Madrid: Cinterco, 1990.

Bohórquez Casado, Manuel. *La Niña de los Peines en la Casa de los Pavón*. Sevilla: Signatura, 2000.

Bois, Mario. *Carmen Amaya: O la Danza del Fuego*. Madrid: Espasa Calpe, 1994.

Boyd, Carolyn P. *Historia Patria: Politics, History, and National Identity*. Princeton, NJ: Princeton University Press, 1997.

Cadena Sur/Radio Sevilla. *150 Años de Feria en Sevilla*. Sevilla: Cadena Sur/Radio Sevilla, 1996.

Campbell, Karen. "With María Benítez in Santa Fe." *Attitude: The Dancers' Monthly* 3, no. 5 (April 1985): 9.

Cancionero de la Niña de la Puebla. Barcelona: Alas, n.d.

Carr, Raymond. *Spain 1808–1975*. 2nd ed. Oxford: Clarendon, 1982.

Casanovas, José. *Manuel de Falla, Cien Años*. Barcelona: Nuevo Arte Thor, 1976.

Castro, Estrellita. *Mi Vida*. Madrid: Astros, 1943.

Chávez, Fray Angélico. "Our Lady of the Conquest." In *Que Vivan las Fiestas*, ed. Donna Pierce, 18–29. Santa Fe: Museum of New Mexico Press, 1985.

———. *The Lady from Toledo: An Historical Novel in Santa Fe*. 1960; rpt., Santa Fe, NM: Friends of the Palace Press, 1993.

Chávez, Thomas E. "Santa Fe's Own: A History of Fiesta." In *Que Vivan las Fiestas*, ed. Donna Pierce, 6–17. Santa Fe: Museum of New Mexico Press, 1985.

Chuse, Loren. *Las Cantaoras: Music, Gender and Identity in Flamenco Song*. New York: Routledge, 2003.

Cristóbal, Ramiro. *Homenaje en su Centenario: Antonia Mercé, "La Argentina," 1890–1990*. Madrid: Ministerio de Cultura, Instituto Nacional de las Artes Escénicas y de la Musica, 1990.

Crow, Jim A. *Spain: The Root and the Flower: An Interpretation of Spain and the Spanish People*. Berkeley: University of California Press, 1985.

de Baca, Juliet C. "Olé Vicente." *New Mexico Magazine*, March 1967.

Delgado, Juan Fabian. *El Cine*. Sevilla: Grupo Andaluz, 1981.

Diaz de Escovar, Narciso. *Nuevos Cantares*. Barcelona: Maucci, 1926.

Dohme, Ralph. "Real Flamenco Hits Santa Fe." *Santa Fe New Mexican*, June 1966.

Draegin, Lois. "Fanning the Spanish Fever." *Dance Magazine*, 1978.

Escribano, Antonio. *Y Madrid Se Hizo Flamenco*. Madrid: El Avapiés, 1990.

Ekstein, Modris. *Rites of Spring: The Great War and the Birth of the Modern Age*. Garden City, NY: Doubleday, 1989.

Elson, Oliva. "Flamenco Continues to Take Japan by Storm." http://www.spanish-teaching.com/2010/8/flamenco-continues-to-take-japan-by-storm (accessed September 21, 2011).

Escudero, Vicente. *Mi Baile*. Barcelona: Muntaner y Simón, 1947.

Falla, Manuel de. *Cante Jondo: El Canto Primitivo Andaluz*. Granada: Uranía, 1922.

Fernández, James D. "Poets, Peasants, Painters, Professors and Performers in New York." In *When Spain Fascinated America*, ed. María López Diaz and Margarita Ruyra de Andrade, 25–45. Zumaia, País Vasco, Spain: Fundación Zuloaga, 2010.

Festival Flamenco Internacional de Albuquerque. Program, Heritage Hotels and Resorts, June 8–14, 2014.

"Fiesta Is a Big Event." *Alamogordo Daily News*, May 11, 1981.

Fisher, Nora. "Costume Equals Festive Fiesta." In *Que Vivan las Fiestas*, ed. Donna Pierce, 18–29. Santa Fe: Museum of New Mexico Press, 1985.

"Flamenco for Culture." *Farmington Daily Times*, October 12, 1980.

"Flamenco Dance Festival Slated at UNM." *Albuquerque Tribune*, July 16, 1987: B7.

"Flamenco <AP>87: Dancers Descend for Workshops, Celebration." *Albuquerque Journal*, July 19, 1987.

"Flamenco Group Performs at Museum." *Santa Fe New Mexican*, September 2, 1966.

"Flamenco Spotlighted at Fiesta." *Santa Fe New Mexican*, September 3, 1967.

"Friday Night Entertainment at La Fonda," *Santa Fe New Mexican*, September 8, 1942.

Friedler, Sharon E., and Susan B. Glazer, eds. *Dancing Female: Lives and Issues of Women in Contemporary Dance.* Amsterdam: Harwood Academic, 1997.

García, Uriel J. "Cave of Creativity." *Santa Fe New Mexican,* February 2, 2014.

García Redondo, Francisca. *El Círculo Mágico: En el Centenario de Antonia Mercé, Vicente Escudero y Pastora Imperio.* Cáceres: Institución Cultural "El Brocense," 1988.

Gibson, Ian. *The Death of Lorca.* London: Allen, 1973.

La Gitana Studio of Dancing Mid-Term Recital. Program, Lensic Theater, February 14–15, 1941.

Graebner, Jim. "*Feria* Needs Change." *New Mexico Daily Lobo,* May 4, 1973.

Graham, Helen, and Jo Labanyi, eds. *Spanish Cultural Studies: An Introduction: The Struggle for Modernity.* Oxford: Oxford University Press, 1995.

Grande, Felix. *Memoria del Flamenco.* Madrid: Espasa Calpe, 1979.

———. *Memoria del Flamenco.* 2nd ed. Barcelona: Círculo de Lectores, Galaxia Gutenberg, 1995.

Greco, José, with Harvey Ardman. *The Gypsy in My Soul: The Autobiography of José Greco.* Garden City, NY: Doubleday, 1977.

Greene, Patterson. "Greco Dance Troupe Clicks." *Los Angeles Examiner,* August 29, 1953.

Guererro, Dolores Pantoja. "Heroínas del Cante." *La Nueva Alborea (Revista de la Agencia Andaluza para el Desarollo del Flamenco),* no. 7 (July–September 2008): 62–64.

Guitar, Lorca, and Flamenco. Playbill, Los Alamos Opera Guild, August 26, 1963.

Gulati, Richa. "Far East Flamenco: Japan's Spanish Dance Scene." *Dance Magazine,* November 2008.

Hayes, Michelle Heffner. *Flamenco: Conflicting Histories of the Dance.* Jefferson, NC: McFarland, 2009.

Holguín, Sandie. *Creating Spaniards: Culture and National Identity in Republican Spain.* Madison: University of Wisconsin Press, 2002.

Hontanilla, Ana. "Images of Barbaric Spain in Eighteenth-Century British Travel Writing." *Studies in Eighteenth-Century Culture* 37 (2008): 119–143.

Iglesias Hermida, Prudencio. *España: El Arte, el Vicio y la Muerte.* Madrid: Imprenta de Juan Pueyo, 1914.

"Juan Siddi Flamenco, Santa Fe." *Santa Fe Now: The City of Santa Fe Event Calendar,* July 17, 2014.

June, Ana. "I Am Flamenco." *Local Flavor*, July 2010: 13–15.

Kagan, Richard L. "The Spanish Craze: The Discovery of Spanish Art and Culture in the United States." In *When Spain Fascinated America*, ed. María López Diaz and Margarita Ruyra de Andrade, 25–45. Zumaia, País Vasco, Spain: Fundación Zuloaga, 2010.

Kern, Robert. *The Regions of Spain: A Reference Guide to History and Culture*. Westport, CT: Greenwood, 1995.

"Kicking Up Her Heels." *Albuquerque Journal*, May 17, 1987.

King, Scottie. "The Two Sides of María Benítez." *New Mexico Magazine*, June 1976: 26–27.

Labanyi, Jo. "The American Connection." In *The Spanish Night: Flamenco, Avant-Garde and Popular Culture 1865–1936*, ed. Patricia Molins and Pedro G. Romero, 91–113. Madrid: Museo Nacional Centro de Arte Reina Sofía, 2008.

Larrea, Arcadio de. *Guía del Flamenco*. Madrid: Nacional, 1975.

"Local Boy Makes Good." *Santa Fe New Mexican*, March 13, 1966.

López, Antonio. "Chuscales: Guitar Cruncher." *Santa Fe New Mexican, Pasatiempo*, January 8–14, 1999.

López Moya, Diego. *La Argentinita: Libro de Confidencias*. Madrid: Establecimiento Tipográfico J. Yagues, 1913–1920.

———. *Pastora Imperio: Libro de Intimidades*. Madrid: Jaime Rates Martín, 1913–1920.

Lorca, Federico García. *Poema del Cante Jondo*. Madrid: Ulises, 1931.

Los Alamos Arts Council Presents Estampa Flamenca, María Benítez Spanish Dance Company. Playbill, September 20, 1980.

Luján, Nestor, and Xavier Montsalvatge. *La Argentina Vista por José Clara: El Arte y la Epoca de Antonia Mercé*. Barcelona: Horta, 1948.

Machado y Alvarez, Antonio [Demófilo]. *Colección de Cantes Flamencos Recogidos y Anotados por Demófilo*. Sevilla: El Porvenir, 1881.

———. *Colección de Cantes Flamencos Recogidos y Anotados por Demófilo*. 3rd ed. Madrid: Cultura Hispánica, 1975.

Mairena, Antonio. *Las Confesiones de Antonio Mairena*. Sevilla: Publicaciones de la Universidad, 1976.

Manfredi Cano, Domingo. *Cante y Baile Flamenco*. 2nd ed. León, Spain: Everest, 1983.

Massine, Leonide. *My Life in Ballet*. London: Macmillan, 1968.

Matteo. *The Language of Spanish Dance*. Norman: University of Oklahoma Press, 1990.

Mazur, Carole. "Festival Flamenco Stamps in Triumph." *Albuquerque Journal*, July 19, 1987.

McCracken, Ellen. *The Life and Writing of Fray Angélico Chávez: A New Mexico Renaissance Man*. Albuquerque: University of New Mexico Press, 2009.

Mérimée, Prosper. *Carmen and Other Stories*. Oxford: Oxford University Press, 1989.

"Miguel Galvez to Sing Flamenco at Folk Art," *Santa Fe New Mexican* [n.d., clipping found in scrapbook of Jean Critchfield].

Molina, Ricardo. *Obra Flamenca*. Madrid: Demófilo, 1977.

Molina, Ricardo, and Antonio Mairena. *Mundo y Formas del Cante Flamenco*. 3rd ed. Sevilla: Libreria Al-Andalus, 1979.

Molina Fajardo, Eduardo. *Manuel de Falla y el Cante Jondo*. Granada: Universidad de Granada, 1962.

Morca, Teodoro. *Becoming the Dance: Flamenco Spirit*. Taos, NM: Teodoro Morca, 2008.

Murciano, Antonio. *Las Dos Pastoras*. Málaga: El Guadalhorce, 1964.

Murphy, Joy. "Ruben Romero's Gypsy Soul." *New Mexico Magazine*, July 1982.

Museo del Baile Flamenco, ed. *Vicente Escudero: Asentado y Pastueño: Colección de José de la Vega*. Sevilla: Flamencosapiens/Museo del Baile Flamenco, n.d.

"Music and the Fiesta." *New Mexico Music: Our Mission to Inspire, Advance and Promote Musical Culture* 1, no. 4 (September 1947).

"New Mexico Flamenco Festival Rises from the Ashes." *New York Daily News*, June 12, 2014.

El Nido's Patio Flamenco Presents June through August Annually Vicente Romero and His Cuadro Flamenco. Program, n.d., collection of Vivian and Pedro Cuadra.

Nolan, Shelly. "Teo Morca: Modern Maestro of Spanish Dance." *Arabesque: A Magazine of International Dance* 9, no. 2 (July–August 1983): 16–18.

Nuñez de Prado, Gustavo. *Cantaores Flamencos: Historias y Tragedias*. Barcelona: Maucci, 1904.

"Olions Sponsor Ritmo Flamenco Show at Civic." *Los Alamos Monitor*, April 9, 1986.

Ortiz Nuevo, José Luís. *Anica la Piriñaca: Yo Tenia mu Güena Estrella*. Madrid: Hiperión, 1987.

———. *Pepe el de la Matrona: Recuerdos de un Cantaor Sevillano*. Madrid: Demófilo, 1975.

Pacheco, Ana. "Life Filled with Dance." *Santa Fe New Mexican*, July 29, 2012.

Pack, Sasha David. *Tourism and Dictatorship: Europe's Peaceful Invasion of Franco's Spain*. New York: Palgrave Macmillan, 2006.

Payne, Stanley G. "The Reencounter between the United States and Spain after 1898." In *When Spain Fascinated America*, ed. María López Diaz and Margarita Ruyra de Andrade, 25–45. Zumaia, País Vasco, Spain: Fundación Zuloaga, 2010.

Peña, María Luz Gonzalez. *Mujeres de la Escena: 1900–1940*. Madrid: Sociedad General de Autores y Editores, 1996.

Persia, Jorge de. *I Concurso de Cante Jondo 1922–1992: Edición Conmemorativa*. Granada: Manuel de Falla Archives, 1992.

Pierce, Donna, ed. *Que Vivan las Fiestas*. Santa Fe: Museum of New Mexico Press, 1985.

Pikula, Joan. "María Benítez: Estampa Flamenca." *Dance Magazine*, November 1984: 46–50.

Pineda Novo, Daniel. *Antonio Machado y Alvarez, "Demófilo": Vida y Obra del Primer Flamencólogo*. Madrid: Cinterco, 1991.

———. *Juana la Macarrona y el Baile en los Cafés Cantantes*. Cornella de Llobregat: Fundació Gresol Cultural, 1996.

Plata, Juan de la. *Flamencos de Jerez*. Jerez de la Frontera, Spain: Cátedra de Flamencología, 1961.

Poesía: Revista Ilustrada de Información Poética 36 y 37 Número Monográfico Dedicado a Manuel de Falla. Madrid: Ministerio de Cultura, 1991.

Pohren, D. E. *The Art of Flamenco*. Madrid: Society of Spanish Studies, 1990.

———. *Lives and Legends of Flamenco: A Biographical History*. Madrid: Society of Spanish Studies, 1988.

Premartin, Julian. *El Cante Flamenco: Guía Alfabética*. Madrid: Afrodisio Aguado, 1966.

Pritchard, Jane, ed. *Diaghilev and the Ballets Russes 1909–1929*. London: Victoria and Albert, 2012.

Puig-Claramunt, Alfonso, and Flora Albaicín. *El Arte del Baile Flamenco.* Barcelona: Poligrafa, 1977.

Pujol Baulenas, Jordi, and Carlos García de Olalla Maristany. *Carmen Amaya: El Mar Me Enseñó a Bailar.* Barcelona: Almendra Music, 2003.

Quiñones, Fernando. *El Flamenco: Vida y Muerte.* Barcelona: Plaza and Janes, 1971.

Ríos Ruiz, Manuel. *El Gran Libro del Flamenco.* Madrid: Calambur, 2002.

Ríos Ruiz, Manuel, and José Blas Vega. *Diccionario Enciclopédico Ilustrado del Flamenco.* Madrid: Cinterco, 1988.

Rojo Guerrero, Gonzalo. *Mujeres Malagueñas en el Flamenco.* Sevilla: Giralda, 2004.

"Romero Envisions State Dance Tour," *Albuquerque Journal* [n.d., clipping found in scrapbook of Jean Critchfield].

Rosen, D. H. "Flamenco Now Dancing to a Very Different Beat." *Japan Times*, November 5, 2010.

Rosen, Lillie F. "The María Benítez Spanish Dance Company, Joyce Theater, NYC." *Attitude: The Dancers' Monthly* 3, no. 12 (September–November 1986): 24.

Rueda, Salvador. *Flamencqueros (Notas de Color, Año 1892).* Córdoba: Demófilo, 1983.

Salaün, Serge. *El Cuplé (1900–1936).* Madrid: Espasa Calpe, 1990.

Salaün, Serge, and Carlos Serrano. *1900 en España.* Madrid: Espasa Calpe, 1991.

San Román, José Muñoz. "Los Cafés Cantantes de Sevilla." *Revista Mundial* 19 (November 16, 1922).

Schreiner, Claus, ed. *Flamenco: Gypsy Dance and Music from Andalusia.* Portland, OR: Amadeus, 1990.

Serra, Estanislao Alberola. *Mil y un Cantares.* Valencia: Emilo Pascual, 1916.

————. *Mil y un Cantares Más.* Madrid: Sucesores Hernando, 1921.

————. *Soleares y Soleariyas.* Sevilla: Asociación Andalucía, 1925.

Serra, Irene Seco. "The Traditional Costumes of Spain." In *Joaquín Sorolla and the Glory of Spanish Dress*, ed. Molly Skorkin and Jennifer Park, 89–101. New York: Queen Sofía Institute, 2011.

Shikaze, Kyoko. "Flamenco in Japan." *Flamenco World On-Line Magazine*, June 2004. http://www.flamenco-world.com.

Simpson, Michael Wade. "Power Spot: Flamenco in Santa Fe." *Santa Fe New Mexican, Pasatiempo,* July 25–31, 2014.

Smith, Craig. "Mind, Body, Soles." *Santa Fe New Mexican, Pasatiempo*, June 19–25, 2009.

Snyder, Gayle. "Chuscales!" *Local Flavor*, July 2011.

———. "Hear the Heartbeat." *Local Flavor*, March–April 2008, 30–32.

"Spanish Dancer from Brooklyn: Romance in Mexico Spurs Action in Sombrero." *Syracuse Herald Journal* [n.d., clipping found in scrapbook, José Greco Files, New York Public Library for the Performing Arts, Jerome Robbins Dance Division].

"Superb Spanish Dance Set Today at St. John's." *Santa Fe New Mexican*, April 4, 1965.

Swan, Bradford F. "Greco and Troupe Perform at Memorial Auditorium." *Providence Journal*, January 11, 1963.

"Talk of the Area." *Santa Fe New Mexican*, June 23, 1966.

Thiel-Cramér, Barbara. *Flamenco: The Art of Flamenco, Its History and Development until Our Days*. Lindigö, Sweden: Remark, 1991.

Thomas, Ralph. "Always Searching for Beautiful Talent." *Providence Journal*, January 11, 1963.

Thompson, Bea. "Romero Show Gets Hand." *Santa Fe New Mexican*, August 27, 1963.

"Tiny Señoritas Wow <AP>Em." *San Diego Union*, April 21, 1959.

Torea, Lydia, and Patricia Bezunartea. *La Gitana Blanca/The White Gypsy: A Flamenco Memoir*. Phoenix, AZ: Bridgewood, 2008.

"Traditional Spanish Flamenco to Open in Santa Fe with Two of the World's Fastest Rising Stars." *Santa Fe New Mexican*, June 12, 1966.

Triana, Fernando de [Fernando Rodríguez Gómez]. *Arte y Artistas Flamencos*. Madrid: Helénica, 1935.

———. *Arte y Artistas Flamencos*. Madrid: Edición Fascínil de la de 1935, 1986.

———. *Arte y Artistas Flamencos*. 2nd ed. Madrid: Clan, 1952.

"Versatile Latin American." *Dance Magazine*, April 1945: 6–7.

"Vicente Romero Concert Set by LA Opera Guild." *Los Alamos Monitor*, August 1966.

Villalon, Fernando. "Sevilla en 1929." *Gaceta Literaria*, no. 59 (June 1, 1929).

La Voz de Su Amo, Catálogo General de Discos 1929. Barcelona: Compañía del Gramófono, 1929.

La Voz de Su Amo, Catálogo General de Discos 1930. Barcelona: Compañía del Gramófono, 1930.

Vural, Soledad Santiago. "The Mother of New Mexico Flamenco." *Santa Fe New Mexican, Pasatiempo*, July 29–August 4, 2005.

Washabaugh, William. *Flamenco: Passion, Politics and Popular Culture*. Washington, DC: Berg, 1996.

W. B. "Romero Olé." *New Mexico Magazine*, July–August 1970.

Williams, Peter. "Iberia in London 3: Spain via Italy and America." *Dance and Dancers* (August 1959): 14–15.

Woodall, James. *In Search of the Firedance: Spain through Flamenco*. London: Sinclair-Stevenson, 1992.

La Zambra de Santa Fe, Restaurante-Tablao Flamenco. Program, July–August 1971.

Zatanía-Rios, Estela. "100 Years of Carmen Amaya." Paper presented at the Fifth Biennial New Perspectives in Flamenco: History and Research Symposium, Albuquerque, NM, June 8–9, 2014.

Credits

All Museum of International Folk Art collections photography by Blair Clark.

Page 2: Photo courtesy of Janet Borelli.

Page 3: Collection of Lili del Castillo and Luís Campos.

Page 6: Museo de Bellas Artes, Seville, Spain, no. Inv.: CE0756P.

Page 10: Museo del Baile Flamenco.

Page 12: Hispanic Society of America, New York, GRF 40953.

Page 14: Estate of Maurice Seymour and New York Public Library for the Performing Arts, Jerome Robbins Dance Division.

Page 16: Museum of International Folk Art, IFAF Collection, FA.2012.53.51.1-9.

Page 17: Museum of International Folk Art, IFAF Collection, FA.2012.53.51.1-9.

Page 18: Museum of International Folk Art, Gift of Lydia Torea, A.2011.25.1-2.

Page 19: Museum of International Folk Art, A.2011.22.5a-d.

Page 23: (top) Museo del Baile Flamenco.

Page 23: (middle) Museo del Baile Flamenco.

Page 23: (bottom) Museo del Baile Flamenco.

Page 24: Hispanic Society of America, New York.

Page 25: Museo de Bellas Artes Seville, Spain, No. Inv. CE0464P.

Page 27: The Hispanic Society of America, New York.

Page 28: Dallas Museum of Art, Foundation for the Arts Collection, gift of Margaret J. and George V. Charlton in memory of Eugene McDermott.

Page 29: Archivo Manuel de Falla, Granada, Spain.

Page 31: Archivo Manuel de Falla, Granada, Spain.

Page 32: (top left) Museum of International Folk Art, A.2011.22.9.

Page 32: Museum of International Folk Art, A.2011.22.10.

Page 33: (top left) Loan courtesy of Julia Chacón.

Page 33: (bottom right) Museum of International Folk Art, IFAF Collection, FA.1962.22.1a-j. Robbins12.

Page 34: (top) McNay Art Museum, Gift of the Tobin Endowment.

Page 34: (bottom) McNay Art Museum, Gift of the Tobin Endowment.

Page 35: McNay Art Museum Library, Bequest of Mary Lynch Kurtz, by exchange.

Page 36: Museo Néstor , Las Palmas, Gran Canaria, Canary Islands, Spain..

Page 37: Archivo Manuel de Falla, Granada, Spain.

Page 39: (left) Hispanic Society of America, New York, GRF 96628.

Page 39: (right) J. Yaques Publicaciones.

Page 40: (top and bottom) Museo del Baile Flamenco.

Page 41: Museo del Baile Flamenco and José de la Vega.

Page 42: Collection of José Valle Fajardo.

Page 44: Loan courtesy of Vivian and Pedro Cuadra.

Page 46: The Metropolitan Museum of Art, Gift of Sir William Van Horne, 1906.

Page 48: Hispanic Society of America, New York, GRF 91048.

Page 50: (top and bottom) Loan courtesy of Elizabeth Serna Cárdenas.

Page 51: Loan courtesy of Julia Chacón.

Page 52: Museo del Baile Flamenco.

Page 53: Loan courtesy of Elizabeth Serna Cárdenas.

Page 54: New York Public Library for the Performing Arts, Jerome Robbins Dance Division.

Page 55: New York Public Library for the Performing Arts, Jerome Robbins Dance Division.

Page 56: Museo del Baile Flamenco.

Page 58: (left) Photo courtesy of Teo Morca.

Page 58: (right) Photo courtesy of Teo Morca.

Page 59: Photo courtesy of Lydia Torea.

Page 60: (top) Collection of Elizabeth Serna Cárdenas.

Page 60: (bottom) Collection of Elizabeth Serna Cárdenas.

Page 62: Estate of Maurice Seymour and New York Public Library for the Performing Arts, Jerome Robbins Dance Division.

Page 63: (left) Collection of Vivian and Pedro Cuadra, (roght) Private collection.

Page 64: Photo courtesy of Lydia Torea.

Page 66: Museo del Baile Flamenco.

Page 68 Library and Archives, Museum of International Folk Art.

Page 70: (left) Photo courtesy of Remedios Guillén.

Page 70: (right) Photo courtesy of Remedios Guillén.

Page 71: Museum of International Folk Art,(top) T.2015.12.1 (bottom) T.2015.12.2.

Page 72: Museum of International Folk Art A.2011.22.3.

Page 73: (left) Private collection and (right) Museum of International Folk Art, Gift of Robin Martin, A.2011.29.5.

Page 74 (top) Library and Archives, Museum of International Folk Art.

Page 74: (bottom). Museum of International Folk Art, A.2011.22.6a-j.

Page 76: Museo de Bellas Artes, Seville, Spain, No. Inv. DO0953P Donación de la Asociación de Amigos del Museo 1992.

Page 77: (top) Library and Archives, Museum of International Folk Art.

Page 77: (bottom) Furniture and chandelier, Museum of International Folk Art, IFAF Collection, FA.2012.71.1a,b, 2, 3, 4. Hat, Museum of International Folk Art, Gift of Robin Martin, A.2011.29.2; shawl, Museum of International Folk Art, A.1950.7.1.

Page 78: Library and Archives, Museum of International Folk Art.

Page 79: (top) Library and Arvhices, Museum of International Folk Art.

Page 79: (bottom) Museum of International Folk Art, IFAF collection, FA.2014.41.1-7 a-h. Location photo shoot courtesy of Barbara Windom.

Page 80: Photo shoot location courtesy of Barbara Windom.

Page 81: Loan courtesy of Remedios Guillén.

Page 82: Museum of International Folk Art, IFAF collection, FA.2008.71.1,2.

Page 83: Museum of International Folk Art, IFAF collection, FA.2008.71.3-5, earrings FA.2008.36.1v.

Page 85: Hair comb, Museum of International Folk Art, IFAF collection, FA.2008.38.1; Shawl, Museum of International Folk Art, FA.2008.10.1.

Page 86: Hair comb, Museum of International Folk Art, IFAF collection, FA.2008.37.1; shawl, Museum of International Folk Art, FA.2008.10.2.

Page 87: (top) Museum of International Folk Art,,IFAF collection, FA.2008.37.1.

Page 87: (bottom) Museum of International Folk Art, IFAF collection, FA.2013.56.1.

Page 90: (top) New Mexico History Museum and Palace of the Governors Photo Archives, 52415.

Page 91: Collection of Anita Gonzales Thomas.

Page 92: New Mexico History Museum 2003.032.016 & 2003.032.006.

Page 93: New Mexico History Museum and Palace of the Governors Photo Archives, PA–MK–82.16.

Page 94: (top left) Museum of International Folk Art, A.2010.94.1.

Page 94: (top right) Museum of International Folk Art, IFAF collection, FA.2009.22.1.

Page 94: (bottom) New Mexico History Museum and Palace of the Governors Photo Archives, 57610.

Page 95: (left) Photo courtesy of Monica Sosaya Halford.

Page 95: (right) New Mexico History Museum and Palace of the Governors Photo Archives, PA–MA–82.8.

Page 96: Museum of International Folk Art, Gift of Dr. Donna Pierce Smith, A.2014.32.1.

Page 97: Loan courtesy of Elizabeth Serna Cárdenas.80.

Page 98: Photo courtesy of Janet Borelli.

Page 100: Photo courtesy of Elizabeth Serna Cárdenas.

Page 101: Loan courtesy of Elizabeth Serna Cárdenas.

Page 102: Loan courtesy of Elizabeth Serna Cárdenas.

Page 104: Photo courtesy of Lili del Castillo and Luís Campos.

Page 105: Photo courtesy of Vivian and Pedro Cuadra.

Page 106: Loan courtesy of Lili del Castillo and Luís Campos.

Page 107: New Mexico History Museum and Palace of the Governors Photo Archives, 030209.

Page 109: Loan courtesy of Vivian and Pedro Cuadra.

Page 110: Collection of Vivian and Pedro Cuadra.

Page 111: Collection of Lili del Castillo and Luís Campos.

Page 114: (top) Photo courtesy of Lili del Castillo and Luís Campos.

Page 114: (bottom) Photo courtesy of Lili del Castillo and Luís Campos.

Page 115: Loan courtesy of Lili del Castillo and Luís Campos.

Page 117: Photo courtesy of María Benítez.

Page 118: Photo courtesy of Lili del Castillo and Luís Campos.

Page 120: Photo courtesy of María Benítez.

Page 121: (top) Museum of International Folk Art, A.2011.22.7.

Page 121: (bottom) Museum of International Folk Art,, A.2011.22.8.

Page 122: Museum of International Folk Art, A.2011.22.2.

Page 123: Museum of International Folk Art, A.2011.22.4a,b.

Page 124: Museum of International Folk Art, IFAF Collection, skirt FA.2012.56.1, shawl FA.1976.65.1.

Page 127: (top) Photo courtesy of Dr. David Briggs.

Page 127: (bottom), Photo courtesy of Giovanna Tema.

Page 129: Collection of Lili del Castillo and Luís Campos.

Page 131: (left and right), Private collection.

Page 132: Museo del Baile Flamenco, Seville, Spain.

Page 133: Museo del Baile Flamenco, Seville, Spain.

Page 134: Collection of Lili del Castillo and Luís Campos.

Page 135: (top) Photo courtesy of Janet Borelli.

Page 135: (bottom), Photo courtesy of Dr. David Briggs.

Page 136: Loan courtesy of Lili del Castillo and Luís Campos.

Page 138: Photo courtesy of Janet Borelli.

Page 140: (top) Photo courtesy of Janet Borelli.

Page 140: (bottom), Photo courtesy of Janet Borelli.

Page 141: Photo courtesy of Janet Borelli.

Page 142: Collection of Teo Morca.

Page 144: Photo courtesy of Hubert Worley.

Page 145: (top and bottom) Photo courtesy of Artotems Co.

Page 146: Photo courtesy of Morgan Smith.

Page 147: Photo coutesty of Morgan Smith.

Page 148: (top and bottom) Photo courtesy of Morgan Smith.

Page 149: Photo courtesy of Tim Jones.

Page 150: Photo courtesy of Mary Nellie Brown.

Page 151: Collection of Lili del Castillo and Luís Campos.

Page 152: Photo courtesy of Andrew John Cecil.

Page 152: Photo courtesy of Andrew John Cecil.

Page 153: Photo courtesy of Victoria Lenihan.

Page 154: Photo courtesy of Morgan Smith.

Page 155: Photo courtesy of Morgan Smith.

Page 157: Private collection.

Page 158: Photo courtesy of Mitsuyo Katsuta.

Page 159: Photo courtesy of Toshinobu Hori.

Page 160: Library and Archives, Museum of International Folk Art.

Page 161: Private collection.

Index

Page numbers in italic refer to illustrations.

Cansino, José, 57–58, 103
cantaoras, 30, 34, 78, 112–13, 126
Cárdenas, Betty Serna, 59, *60*, 93, *97*, *100*, 102–03, 112
Carmen (Bizet), 13, 133
Carmen (Mérimée), 12–13, 61
Carmen (movie), 133, *134*
Carmencita, *46*, 47, 65
Carmencita (Chase), *46*, 47
Carnela, Daniel, *86*, 87
Casa de la Memoria, 156
caseta de feria, 75, *76*, 77, 78, 84
castanets, 15, 36, *51*, 60, 65, 93, 97, *100*, 103, 105, 152
Castillo, Lili del, 8, 97, 103, *104*, 108, 113, *114*, 125–26, 130, *150*, *151*
caves. *See* Sacromonte caves (Granada)
Centro Andaluz de Documentación del Flamenco, 155
Chacón, Julia, *150*
Chase, William Merritt, *46*, 47
Chávez, Fray Angélico, 95
Chávez, Nora, 93
Choly and Isabel, 8, *111*
Chuscales, 42, 143, *146*, 154
Concurso del Cante Jondo, 30, 34
concursos, 30, 34, 56–57, 69, 142, 156
Conservatory of Flamenco Arts, 141–43
Coral, Matilde, 65
costumbrismo, 24–25
costumes, 24, 57, 65, 80, *136*
    alpargatas (espadrilles), 17
    bullfighter's, *14*, 15, *32*, *33*, 47
    china poblana, 93
    competitions for, 78, 91
    faldas (skirts), *18*, 122
    Florinda, 45
    regional, *16*, *17*, *18*, *19*, 25, 93, 95
    shawls, *82*, *83*, *92*, 93, *96*, *101*
    slippers, *14*, 15
    torero, 11, 147
    traje campero, 70, 74, 75
    traje de gitana, *70*, *72*, 75
    traje de luces, 47
    traje de volantes, 75, 80, *91*
    traje flamenca, 122, *123*
    vests, *121*.
    See also batas de cola; *mantóns de Manila*; *peines*
Cuadra, Vivian Alarid, *104*
cuadro, 24, 33, 57
Cuadro Flamenco, 30, 57
Culbert, Peter, 130

Dalí, Salvador, 30, 38, 49
Dance and Dancers magazine, 63
dance festivals, 57, 119–20, 128. *See also* specific festivals
Dance Magazine, 52, 61, *124*, 125
dance training, 38, 50
    in academies/studios, 24, 102–03, 128–29
    in Spain, 43, 103, 107, 112–13, 116–17, 143, 146–47, 150–51, 156, 160.
    See also specific programs; specific studios
de Falla, Manuel, 30, *31*, 35, 37, 42, 48–49, 57

de Geus, Lucilene, *149*, 150
de la O, Cristobal, 129
de la Rosa, Felipe, *114*, 119
de la Torre, Néstor Martín-Fernández, 30, *36*
de la Vega, Alejandro, *52*
Denishawn School of Dancing and Related Arts, 57–58
Diaghilev, Sergei, 30
Diaz, María. *See* Benítez, María
duende, 22
Duran, Carla, 8, 109, *111*

Edison, Thomas, 47, 65
El Amor Brujo, 30, *31*, 37–38, 48–49, 133
El Burrero *café cantante*, 24–26
El Café de Chinitas, 38, 49, 51
El Chavalillo, 116
El Kursaal Central café, 27
El Nido restaurant, 7–8, 109–14, 117–20, 125–26, 152, 160
El Niño Brillante, 106
El Niño Dorado, 112–13
El Tricornio, 30, 34
Elssler, Fanny, 45, 47
Enciñias, Joaquín, 139, *140*, 141–42
Enciñias, Marisol, 139, *140*, 141–43
Enciñias-Sandoval, Eva, 128, *129*, 130, *131*, 134, *135*, 139, *140*, 141–42, 146
Entreflamenco, 149
Escudero, Vicente, 37, 38–39, 40, *41*, 49, 61
Española, New Mexico, 84, *100*
Estampa Flamenca: María Benítez Teatro Flamenco. *See* Teatro Flamenco
Estancia Alegre, Alcalde, New Mexico, 79, *80*
Eugenia, Victoria, 116
Europe, 24, 26, 36, 38, 47, 49, 57, 61, 97, 108

Fajardo, José Valle, 42, 143. *See also* Chuscales
Fajardo, Mina Valle, *146*, 154, 156
Ferdinand, King, 21
Feria, 125
Feria de Abril, 69–70, *71*, 75–76, 77, 78, 89
Feria de San Miguel, 75
ferias (fairs), *68*, 155
    costumes for, 70, *72*, *73*, 74, 75, 78, *81*, *82*, *83*, 160
    description of, 7, 69–70, 75–76, 80, 84
Fernández, Eddie, 58, *59*
Festival Flamenco, *111*, 126
Festival Flamenco Internacional de Albuquerque, 8–9, 98, 130, *131*, *132*, 134, *135*, *136*, *138*, 139, *140*, 141–43, 146, 153, 156
festivals, 8, 76. *See also* ferias (fairs); fiestas; specific festivals
Fiesta de Los Angeles, 89
Fiesta de Santa Fe, 90, 102, 111–12, 120, 143
    costumes for, 89, 91, *92*, 93, *94*, 95, *96*, 97
    description of, 8, 84, 89, 91, 97
Fiesta de Taos, 97, 116
Fiesta del Caballo, 70, 79
Fiesta en una Caseta (Bejarano), 76
fiestas, 8, 11, 25, 36, 43, 56, 84, 99–100, 139, 155.
    See also specific fiestas
flamenco
    alegría, 137

Project editor: Mary Wachs
Design and production: David Skolkin
Composition: Set in Scala and Akkurat
Manufactured in China
10 9 8 7 6 5 4 3 2 1

Cataloging-in-Publication Data
Library of Congress Cataloging-in-Publication Data

Chávez, Nicolasa (Nicolasa M.)
  The spirit of flamenco : from Spain to New Mexico / by Nicolasa Chávez.
     pages cm
  Includes bibliographical references and index.
  ISBN 978-0-89013-608-9 (hardcover : alk. paper) 1. Flamenco. 2. Flamenco—Spain.
3. Flamenco—New Mexico. 4. Flamenco—United States. I. Title.
  GV1796.F55C435 2015
  793.3'19468--dc23
                              2015014662

Museum of New Mexico Press
PO Box 2087
Santa Fe, New Mexico 87504
mnmpress.org